MONET

Jean-Jacques Lévêque

MONET

CRESCENT BOOKS
NEW YORK

Translated from the French by *Carol Lee Rathman*

This 1990 edition published by Crescent Books,
distributed by Crown Publishers, Inc., 225 Park Avenue South,
New York, New York 10003.

Printed and bound in Italy

ISBN 0-517-69480 8

h g f e d c b a

Table of contents

INDEX OF ILLUSTRATIONS

AGAINST PERMANENCY

Many are the dictators who have sought to enhance their popularity and prestige by assigning to art the task of immortalizing their regimes. Some rulers showed more flair than others in their choice of artists; Louis XIV, by surrounding himself with a court of artists and writers at Versailles and Napoleon, by entrusting the revolutionary David with the prodigious task of creating a style that would bear his name, were no doubt better counseled than Napoleon III, whose official painters are now viewed, with some indulgence, as prime examples of social decadence. These "pompiers" (stuffed shirts), as they were so deliciously dubbed, came and went freely at the Tuileries; they strutted about at the fêtes given in their honor; they received medals and premiums and honors of all sorts. They remained closed in their studios where they frequently received calls from the *cocottes*, their neighbors in the court on the side bordering the Monceau plain and Boulevard Péreire.

Carried away with their artistic canons, their self-importance and their success, they let the painting be done elsewhere: in the streets or the great outdoors.

When Napoleon appointed Count Nieuweskerke Superintendent of the Fine Arts, the latter's ideas became official policy; they can be summed up by the count's vehement assertion with reference to the Barbizon school, that he had "no love for this art of the people, for these men who do not even change their undergarments".

There is a clear difference between those who uphold false values and those who venture into the unexplored realms of the sensibilities. It was a bitter struggle in which the rich, ensconced in the stronghold of the Salon, repulsed the repeated assaults of the innovators (beggars, they were considered) who, tired of this constant rejection, were gathering force. Napoleon III, in a demagogic *beau geste*, proposed the establishment of an alternative salon, the Salon des Refusés. It was only a half-measure and showed a gross error in judgment, in view of the great uproar

Monet started out his career as a caricature artist.

Young Woman with Pointed Nose.

Eugène Scribe.

Ursule Cellerier.

Portrait, presumed to be of Victor Hugo.

J.F. Félix Huson.

The Pianist.

Théodore Pelloquet.

Jules de Primaray.

that it caused. It also foreshadowed the Nazi's decision, equally misguided, to exhibit the Expressionists and other artists representing decadent movements alongside the artists recognized by the regime, to highlight the *difference*. Despotic regimes always count on the support of bigots, and often it is the mission of innovative art to exterminate them. It is of course an explosive situation.

This adventure (and its outcome) always works to the favor of the outcasts who head up the revolt.

A VAGABOND

Already as a child Monet showed his deepset instinct for wandering. He was a little ragamuffin roaming the great outdoors, playing on the beach, skipping school. An incurable truant, he had only the bare rudiments of an education. He preferred direct contact with nature. He was always an outdoors man. Well-being, for him, consisted in the thrill of physical freedom that one feels when in harmony with the environment. He was never one for ponderous reflection or cumbersome cultural baggage; rather he worked from instinct, spontaneity, impressions.

He exuded an irrepressible energy. All those who have described him have mentioned his calm self-assurance.

Gustave Geffroy speaks of a "hale, rugged man, bearded and wearing heavy boots, rough canvas clothes, a sailor's cap over his eyes, a wooden pipe stuck in his thick beard".

What emerges, in sum, is the portrait of a captain of the high seas. Marc Elder, much later, sketched out a "typical gardener, thickset and steady". These are not insignificant observations. On land or on water, Monet was solidly anchored to nature, a willing figurehead, and through it he was able to rid his images of all the inexactness and artistic expedience that could muddle it. At the same time, underlying this solidity was all the finesse of the subtlest sensations, just as underlying the bold impact of a physical approach straight from nature was a painting style that far from treating reality as a certainty shattered it and projected all its calm energy into the realm of uncertainty. Some observers have been too hasty in confining Monet's experience to that of the Impressionist group, even if he was undeniably its leading light; the fact remains that he defies all the theoretical definitions that underpin group activity. Theories seem to be made for those who by nature need to belong.

Monet was a loner. He was not at all sparing in his friendships and personal exchanges, but he had a deep-seated need for solitude. His work evolved

16

differently from that of thc Impressionists, even though paradoxically it expressed the group's boldest conquests.

Regardless of the group's formation (in 1886), Monet pursued his own personal experience. As it accelerated and expanded, he reached the newest and most complex realms of the visual as much in terms of artistic insight as technique.

Monet's refinement of his own pictorial language is the reason behind the broad range of interpretations – of the most contradictory nature – that he is subject to. By turns a painter of a world in the present, of bliss, of passing time, of primal emotions, of matter in movement, of the ineffable, he swung from realism towards unreality, from the solid world towards an atomized space, from calm stability towards decomposition as much of reality as of a boundless sensation.

BOUDIN'S LESSON

Alone in his remote province (a setting that reeked of Bovary) as Monet sought a teacher who would introduce him to the art of painting, he risked falling into the grips of one of those skilful technicians who was sure of his means and faithful to the canons, but limited by a narrow outlook and an academic spirit. His fortune, and it was extraordinary considering the great headstart it gave him, was to have found as his first guide the painter Boudin. Strangely, at first Monet avoided him, fled from him. But the encounter was destined to happen, thanks to the persistence of the picture framer engaged by Monet for his caricatures and by Boudin for his canvases. The meeting took place and the seduction plot worked. Boudin's ideas stimulated Monet. He told his student to be "extremely stubborn about capturing the raw impression, which is the right one. [...] Anything that is painted right on the spot shows an energy, a power, a liveliness of touch that cannot be recreated in the studio", and again, in his slogan-like turn of phrase, "three strokes of the brush done from life are worth more than two days of work in the studio". Of course, he took Monet along with him on his pilgrimages "to the motif", to the beach, before a sea that was forever changing, that unlike the majestic and sometimes disquieting fixity of the Mediterranean, its unblemished expanse echoed by the sky (which inspired abstraction), showed an agitation, a diversity, a richness of nuance that highlighted the particular. These qualities led Boudin to a slight over-attention to detail and a sharp emphasis on the figures, and soon led Monet to a no less lively fragmentation that was to form the basis of Impressionism.

In addition to introducing Monet to nature, Boudin initiated him to a particular notion of "quest", the awakening to the gap between knowing what one wants and then being able to achieve it. This was in a period when painting was self-taught, when formulas circulated from atelier to atelier, and it was believed that they could be mastered only thanks to an innate ability.

Boudin. *Beach at Trouville.*
The Phillips Collection.

The Beach at Trouville. 1870.
London, Tate Gallery.
A style close to Manet's.

The Hève Point at Low Tide. 1865.
Fort Worth, The Kimbell Art Museum.
His familiarity with the seasides of France made the painter into a keen
observer of the hardworking lifestyle there.

Instead, Boudin taught Monet that the language of painting was entirely to be invented. From the very start he gave painting a new dimension: that of adventure. In the hotel-ateliers of the glorified "pompiers" (stuffed shirts, official artists), it was forbidden to ask questions, while Monet and his friends did nothing but ask them. And in fact, since then, artists have continued to place the accent on the searching aspect of art, on specific aims, and no longer view it as an experience transmitted from generation to generation. What may have been true as long as art was restricted to the studio, as long as it did not venture beyond the bounds of this theatre set up by the painter who transferred to the canvas only what he had established within the space of his studio, could no longer apply to an art that had ventured beyond, into nature.

At the same time, the paint itself, the chemical composition of which had remained altered for generations, underwent a change: it was now sold in easily transportable tubes. This pushed painters out of their studio-factories – heavy, stationary pieces of equipment, where artists "turned out" paintings according to time-proven formulas, often with the help of assistants.

Standing alone before a quivering, changing nature, the painter found that traditional techniques were totally unsuited to translating life. He could no longer paint conventional images, but had to transmit to the canvas, for example, the fleeting passage of a cloud as it inscribed in absolute space its shadowplay.

Painting shifted from a conceptual, strictly intellectual activity to something living and actually experienced, from a static, frozen image to a constantly changing, moving reality. This reality was even emotionally stirring: the painters who sought to capture it could not resist interpreting it as well, despite their claims to the contrary, adding the impression it aroused in them as they stood naked before it, observing it. In effect, their aim was to make the transience of a moment coexist with the even

25

greater evanescence of the impression received in this fragment of time, beyond the grasp of whomever is not finely tuned into the deep-flowing currents of his own sensibility. Studio painting merely required the skilful manipulation of the tools available, but for the artist who ventured into the indescribable, these tools were useless. All of modern art evolved as a function of the ambition, at the time quite new, to turn painting into the handwriting of the sensibilities; painting could no longer follow the dictates of convention, fashion, and trends to produce mere illustration.

With Monet and those who came after him, the painter worked with the paradox of honing the present down until it shattered, at the same time completely merging his thoughts and sensation into the object painted, with sensation prevailing over observation. Not that the latter was abandoned or overlooked; it was simply no longer a heavy petrified element of the image, since reality was discovered to be not immobile, static, dead, but so alive that each instant is unique. And elusive. Sometimes making sensation prevail over observation was taken to a tragic extreme: it was what thrust van Gogh, for example, towards his death, because he gradually let his emotive, "moved" self replace the reality that gave rise to this emotion. Monet attained this sublime dimension of painting by no longer expressing the down-to-earth reality, but rather reality in all its immensity, its perceptible, imaginative totality. Thus Monet brought to western art the dreamy elastic perspective which he identified with, and which in Eastern art was the tradition.

29

BARBIZON AND CO.

Though Monet's studies at Gleyre's atelier – where he met Bazille, Renoir and Sisley – yielded him nothing, he did not turn to the museums for help. He fled the atelier, where the masters taught how nature could be "corrected" according to traditional canons of art. For the very same reason, Manet fled Thomas Couture's atelier. But Manet made a standing jump; he reached out towards the Spanish or Flemish traditions for his inspiration, copying Franz Hals' work. Monet instead advocated a direct confrontation with nature. This is what made him more revolutionary than his colleagues. Of course, he too at times turned to various artists for inspiration: the intimism of Corot, for example, the bold perspicacity of Boudin, the sensual realism of Courbet, the verve of Jongkind – all artists with whom hc fclt a dircct affinity and whom hc held in friendly regard.

Manet, the cultured dandy, studied at the Louvre, while Monet, an alumnus of the school of truancy, preferred the thickets of the Fontainebleau forest.

From the very outset, even while he was still receptive to influences which he digested and adapted, he was an ardent believer in the *plein air* technique.

Even Cézanne, a future companion in travels and in battle, took his first steps in the direction of history, despite his narrow provincialism, his misanthropy, and his unsociability. He consulted with the past and gauged his work on the basis of this experience; hence, his famous ambition of "doing Poussin from life".

Monet's initial force lay in his having confronted reality without passing through the intermediary of museum culture. The little vagabond who had roved over the shores of his youth must have acquired the keen visual – as well as imaginative – sensibility that led him to the bold discoveries of the Impressionists. Others were to arrive at the same conclusion through a series of reactions, but Monet was guided and inspired by a natural impulse.

Déjeuner sur l'herbe.
Moscow, Pushkin Museum.

Manet. *Déjeuner sur L'Herbe.*
London, Courtauld Institute.

Manet. *Portrait of Monet.*

(overleaf) *Camille.* 1866.
Bern, Kunsthalle.
The sensual splendour of the fabrics.

35

He returned to the forest of Fontainebleau with his new friends, counting among them Bazille, because there he found a natural truth that eclipsed all academic lessons. He was not hung up on a past about which he had no knowledge and he even ignored. This sort of virginity was an asset to him. His instinct was so sure and so strong that he could not have felt totally at ease in a terrain favorable to so many others: the intensity of the shadows, the harshness of the color contrasts between clearing and deep underbrush determined a "heavy" style of painting with thickly applied paints. Monet was more familiar with boundless spaces, a radiant, glowing light that washed over marine expanses. The Fontainebleau forest taught him about nature, but it still had not revealed itself to him in all of its greatness. He approached this site listening to Courbet's counsels, but he had neither the latter's heavy sensuality nor his resonant volubility. His interpretation of the forest was therefore a little stiff and reticent, and it did not escape a certain propriety. One senses that the painter was still holding himself back.

Nevertheless, he worked exclusively "on location", unlike the Barbizon painters who did not object to finishing – if not inventing – their landscapes in the studio. He approached his painting free of cultural prejudices – unlike Manet, for example, whom he had just discovered and whose fresh and open-handed way of distributing light and shadow within the space of the canvas he admired.

This did not mean that he sought to emulate the other. The definitive proof of this comes from an ambitious canvas he was undertaking in this period on the theme of "Le Déjeuner sur l'Herbe".

For Monet, it was a question of representing the figures just as they appeared to him in the natural light against a backdrop of greenery.

He carefully chose the clearing that suited him, and positioned the objects and people in it, since he was determined not to hedge on the truth, or better to arrive at truth by remaining utterly dependent on it.

Total realism. Monet was thus at an essential crossroads in the history of art where, aiming at absolute realism he prepared to plunge painting into its deliquesence. It was a long road set out before him, and his lifework shows the steps he took along it, a long but unescapable metamorphosis of the language of art, which once caught up with the truth then surpassed it, arriving at an internalized vision of things, though his sole ambition had been to remain faithful to the most subtle appearances of these things. In fact, his *Déjeuner sur l'Herbe* had a more radical impact on the future of painting than Manet's version. Manet still believed in the canons of museum art, in a past which he challenged and in a culture whose laws he was out to break, all the while recognizing its validity and admitting the tyranny of a heritage. Manet flouted taboo, while Monet sharpened his gaze.

Paradoxically, it was Manet who shocked. Monet offered an apparently admissible, reasonable work that reflected the mood of the times, but which already foreshadowed the great revolution that would rock painting down to our own times.

It was such a respectable realism that it merited the attention of even the most resistant to change. And the canvas that he presented at the 1866 Salon, the *Portrait of Camille* (painted immediately after the *Déjeuner sur l'Herbe*) may have seemed innocuous even to the spirits most averse to initiative. The realism was so complete that Zola, who fashioned himself the champion of realism, sang in praise of its successful rendering of "each detail without having lapsed into aridity. Look at the robe, how supple and solid it is, how softly it trails, it lives, it says out to words out loud who this woman is. This is not a doll's gown or one of those chiffon rags that dress dreams".

The Chailly-en-Bière owner of the *Déjeuner sur l'Herbe* abandoned it at a pawnbroker's to pay off a debt. Later, the painter himself found it mouldering in an attic, and destroyed it. He had planned to present this canvas at the 1866 Salon, but instead the choice fell to the *Portrait of Camille*. This all goes to show the unfortunate fate of a painting which, destined to the Salon, Monet had carried out following the advice of Courbet. He later did a copy of it that was more in line with his initial ambitions.

With his *Women in the Garden*, Monet furthered his experiments. For him, the problem was simple: to find the right tone, the truth of an instant, in lighting effects. This led him to paint only under given climactic conditions – and this was a habit he kept for life. Courbet once met Monet as he was working on the portrait in Ville d'Avray, and was surprised to note that the painter waited for the sun to come out again before resuming his work. Monet explained that he did not want to shatter the homogeneity of the light.

Saint-Germain l'Auxerrois. 1867.
Berlin, National Gallery
The Impressionists were also remarkable witnesses of the Paris of their times.

HYMN TO THE CITY

Like Manet, Claude Monet was considered by his contemporaries to be a painter of modern life. Zola said that "he loves the horizons of our cities, with their grey and white patches formed by the buildings against the pale sky; he loves the people in their overcoats on the streets, bustling about their business; he loves racetracks, the fashionable avenues resonant with the sound of traffic; he loves women, their parasols, their gloves, their clothes, even their wigs and facepowder – all that makes them daughters of our civilization".

This remark was made in reference to a series of paintings that has come down to us only in meagre fragments. Many of these "urban" canvases have disappeared; since the years in which he produced them were materially the most difficult ones for the painter, it is easy to imagine that he scraped them down for re-use, or that they were confiscated by creditors or simply forgotten.

Of the Parisian cityscapes of this period, only the view of *Saint-Germain l'Auxerrois*, the *Quai du Louvre*, and the *Playground* have survived. The last of these offers a good example of the technique, then quite innovative, of taking a high-angle view of a place and setting it in a daring perspective, just as photographers were doing at the time. But even more importantly, in the *Playground* the representation of the background to infinity is as precise as that of the foreground. This uniformity, while sacrificing detail, on the other hand offers pictorial accents that capture the dynamism of movement.

In this sense, Monet succeeded admirably in capturing simultaneously the unity of an action, even if complex, and the particular character of each silhouette. Rather than describing them, he confined himself to expressing their dynamism. He chose a fragmented, intense handling, which marks a subject in movement. He had no descriptive aims, which would have broken the unity in favor of a simple accumulation of detail; rather, he was determined to arrive at expressions that combined their effects and through this repetition suggested the movement of a crowd.

Boulevard des Capucines.
Private collection.

Beach at Saint-Adresse. 1867.
Chicago, Art Institute.
The poetry of space.

View of Les Tuileries.
Paris, Musée Marmottan.
A "high-angle" view resembling a cinematographic shot.

The Monceau Park.
New York, Metropolitan Museum of Art.
Pointillism ahead of its time to convey a sense of the heat.

e Playground. 1867.
erlin, Memorial Museum.
photographic framing.

He thus provided the answer to Baudelaire's remark that there is in modern life "a rapidity of movement that demands of the artist equal speed in expression".

Taking up the urban motif again in 1873, when he painted two views of the Boulevard des Capucines looking towards the Opéra, Monet continued to use the technique of the fragmented, swift brushstroke. It was typical of and unique to his experiments in the context of Impressionism, which was just then coming into being. Other milestones were: views of the Tuileries and the Monceau Park in 1876 and then in 1878 and that surprising cityscape entitled *London by Night*, of 1917.

The encoding of visual information in smears of color (this was the technique used in the *Water Lilies* series) that did not fix a shape but underlined its placement in space, has been quite accurately compared to the trail in color photographs left by a light moving through darkness.

Renoir: *La Grenouillère*.
Stockholm, National Museum.

LA GRENOUILLERE

If, according to a current notion, to paint is to show one's inner nature, to freely express oneself, any influence from the past can only be seen as negative.

Hardly a release for the painter, he cannot be himself until he has shed his randomly acquired and "self"-compromising cultural baggage. The more he is burdened with cultural references and models, the longer it will take him to become aware of his true self.

While the painter working on commission for a patron who above all expected craftsmanship from him had to look to the past, to seek formulae, the painter as we conceive him today must, to the contrary, remove himself from the amalgam of the past, which can only be a hindrance.

One can see how van Gogh, for example, discovered himself in the midday sun in the same moment as he forgot J.F. Millet, whom he must have imitated as he was starting out.

This gestation, painful for many, is generally accompanied by spectacular psychological rejection mechanisms, as if the painter were killing his father, all a part of the dynamics of rebellion. All of painting since the 19th century has been a succession of rejections of the past.

Nothing of the kind appears in Monet's case, since he was not at all encumbered by any sort of cultural baggage. His artistic sensibilities were untouched by ideas in conflict with his aspirations. The successive contributions of Boudin, Jongkind and Courbet were catalysts that made him progressively more aware of himself.

His friendly, intimate relationship with Renoir, on the other hand, helped to strengthen his intuition. In 1869-70 the rudiments of his style, a rigorous fragmentation, began to appear in his work, preparing the way for the Impressionist technique.

"La Grenouillère" was an open air café like many of its time, all casually lined up along the banks of the Seine, where people engaged in water sports. It was not far from where Guy de Maupassant found some of the character models for his most vivid and

cruel stories. These places were great melting pots of a humanity with a very free lifestyle; they made up a vast psychological arena where the writer could find abundant and rich material. Monet approached them only as a painter: never even dreaming of trying to enrich his canvas with the anecdotal, he radically detached himself from the human to achieve a strictly atmospheric space.

The water, the trees, a light, the shadows, the fig-
ures are all there only as dynamic points in a shimmering, unstable open space.

Painting became a moment suspended in time, where a tangible, identifiable reality is expressed along with the forces of a nature that has been brought to life by the light and by the painter's handling which in itself makes up another layer of meaning. Vibrant, intense brushstrokes placed side by side speak of the painter's vigor as well as of his emotions.

MADE IN ENGLAND

Monet was with Camille and their son Jean in Trouville – where he had met up with Boudin – when France declared war on Germany in July of 1870.

Some landscapes dating to this short stay on the Channel coast show how Monet had developed his technique, strengthening it and coming close to that of Manet, large and expressive where the immediacy of the image was joined by its vigor.

For him, it was the end of his painting's "infancy". An enforced stay in England launched him definitively on the path of a truly new style of painting. While he conserved his open-handed style with its sweeping accents in a few London scenes, as he became more familiar with Turner and Whistler he left it behind. With these two artists, the figure dissolves in the light. Following a brief stay in Holland and his return to France, Monet adopted a painting technique with more finely fragmented brushstrokes fusing masses and space into a luminous unity. After his exile in England, Monet decided to settle in Argenteuil. This was the beginning of a long and consistent presence of water in his life; it would henceforth underlie his most important works. His search for objectivity led him to paint the same theme in many different ways, scenes depicted from different angles, or in various kinds of light.

Displacement in time and space, shifting around a central point, was one of the artist's great innovations. He thus got the idea of constructing his "bateau-atelier", his floating studio, the one immortalized in Manet's famous work. In this way, Monet could get to the heart of the elements. One cannot help but recall how his predecessor Turner, whom Monet had just discovered in London, had had himself lashed to the mast of a ship to better understand the sea's motions, to feel through his whole body the mobility of the subject he painted. Jongkind also comes to mind here, with his remark that one could never paint a rushing brook without first having dipped his feet into it, to feel with all his

The Pond at Argenteuil.
Paris, Musée du Louvre.
A strong familiarity with the world of water.

Argenteuil.
Paris, Musée du Louvre.

body the element that he was depicting. What may seem a simple practical solution in fact set a precedent that crystallized a new way of perceiving reality.

The transition from the studio to the "motif", the subject, permitted the painter to get closer to the reality that he was painting, but Monet was not satisfied with what was for him merely a first step; he took a second, much more important step that led him directly into the element itself, to the heart of its special qualities.

In this way he took a more intimate part in the capricious, shifting alliances between the air and the water. He was certainly not yet exclusively captivated by this keen, daring way of seeing things. He worked with various subjects, passing from the river to the city or his private life. Though his bold technique was getting stronger, when he turned to his private life, he knew that he had to restrict himself to the faces, the intimate details, for the sake of a bliss that he seemed to pick up with keen subtlety. Compared to Renoir, his most faithful easel-mate whose painting sang of the flesh, love and pleasure, Monet is more subtle, more discrete: in the space of the instant that he has fixed he makes waves of melancholy pass.

These paintings almost represent a regression with respect to the daring of a work such as *Impression: Rising Sun* of 1873, the key canvas of Monet's career and the banner canvas of the entire Impressionist movement, even if the painter regarded it as a sketch, an outline, an annotation.

It was when the critics saw this painting, presented at the first exhibition of a group of painters who were tired of being rejected by the official Salon, that the name "Impressionism" was coined.

"They are Impressionists inasmuch as they do not paint the landscape but the sensation produced by the landscape". Thus, the "Société anonyme des peintres, sculpteurs et graveurs", as they had until then called themselves, found itself graced with a name. As was frequently the case afterwards, it was a gibe, a word thrown out in derision, that became the bannerhead of a group, of an artistic tendency.

Strangely enough, the works presented at the encounter of April 1874 hosted by Nadar in Boulevard des Capucines were conspicuously lacking in coherence; even Monet's presentation included such diverse works as *Impression: Rising Sun*, *Le Déjeuner* (1868), and *Boulevard des Capucines*, all painted on location.

Did this mean that the Impressionists had not yet set their aesthetic aims in focus?

It was not a matter of theory. Impressionism was in constant development, and the proof of this lay in the many works that slipped beyond the aesthetic control of their authors. It is certain that from Monet's point of view, *Impression: Rising Sun* did not have the importance that the critics afforded it. He had given it its title off-handedly. He later explained that it was simply a painting done from his window in Le Havre to capture the effect of the sun shining through the mist that shrouded the masts of the boats at the docks.

"They asked me its title for the catalogue. It certainly could not be taken for a view of Le Havre, so I said: 'call it *Impression*'."

There has been a lot of talk about Impressionism. At first it was limited to outright mockery, but later people began to consider it the start of a radical transformation of the canons of painting. Monet's art, more than anything else, stands to prove that there was an evolution according to new optical requirements that arose from photography's new role in the field of narrative representation: painting was from that time free to explore the expressive possibilities inherent in the medium itself.

Alongside the purely instinctive lessons of Boudin, Courbet and Jongkind, the English developments in painting had a decisive impact on Monet – this intrepid, solitary explorer of new realms of painting had finally discovered painters who thought like him and who had foreshadowed his ambitions.

Le Déjeuner. 1873.
Paris, Musée du Louvre.
Somewhere between Renoir, for its richness of detail, and Bonnard, for
its atmospheric sensuality.

For example, what Monet discovered and admired in Turner was "this same love for the elusive effect of the hazy, the uncertain; the same romantic passion for the sun, and it is highly likely that the idea of the series owed something to his recollection of the London painter. All that is nebulous in Monet's art – such a divergence from the French tradition – links him to Turner. Furthermore, the fact must not be overlooked that the overall evolution of ideas in France around this time was influenced by an emerging anglomania".

London, the city famous for its fog, must have brought out the seafarer, the man of open maritime spaces in Monet, a way of seeing things that greatly differed from that offered by the French environment to artists whose first steps towards modernity in painting were mostly oriented towards the plant-world.

But Turner, more than Monet would ever be, was attracted to literary references. Though he mined nature down to its elemental stratum for the impulses that he passed on to us in his own way, he was also concerned with a synthesis, a symbolic value that would be later taken up by Redon. Monet, on the other hand, was more direct, more painterly and more absolute in his pictorial choices, and the materiality of his style of expression tended to be an end in itself. Monet likewise distinguished himself from his colleagues with regard to the Japanese influence. While for Manet and Degas Japanese art served as a picturesque accessory in the composition of a painting, for Monet it introduced a new way of "conceiving" nature, of penetrating it, of identifying himself with it to the point of losing his own sense of identity in a form of pantheism that was essentially poetic.

Monet's ambition, which remains surprisingly up-to-date, was to create the bond between meaning and emotion, as opposed to knowledge.

Though Impressionism preached freedom, as practised by Monet this was far from meaning anarchy. He wanted to cast new but fundamental lines

The Dinner. 1868.
Zurich, Fondation Buhrle.
The echoes of a literary tradition that described the family as a pillar of equilibrium.

between the realm of the visible and the painter's consciousness, between the reality and the perceptible. At the same time, he created a steady equilibrium between the universe and a stray particle of consciousness which reached out to become one with the universe, through thought, expression and creation.

In dismissing the picturesque – even human presence was too intrusive for his art – Monet sought to reject all static interference in a vision that achieved its greatest expression in his last large syntheses. These communicate a totality and a state of becoming, a global unity and a vibration whose effect becomes local while still acting in an absolute space.

Just as Mallarmé succeeded in making words elude the banality of their common meaning, bringing them to a new height of sonority, and just as Debussy made musical notes merge into a space of pure harmony, Monet tended towards a style of representation that eluded all pragmatism.

His kind of exoticism did not derive from Japanese art, but from his thought, his impressions, his philosophical and religious orientation.

The body became one with what it felt. It was the incarnation of emotion. The painting was no longer distinct from whomever produced it. It was no longer a commercial object rendered self-sufficient by its own specific qualities. It was a continuum, without a beginning or an end, a long sentence without punctuation, irreducible. The "series" was to be the first consequence of this, the *Water Lilies* its far-reaching effect.

The Japanese Bridge. 1899.
Philadelphia, Museum of Art.
A basic harmony between the water and its green setting.

A CATHEDRAL OF IRON AND SMOKE

In 1877 Monet finally painted the Gare Saint-Lazare as he envisioned it, having formulated the specific problem he wished to address.

He was so taken with his subject that he went to live nearby it, in Rue de Moncey, where Caillebotte had found him an apartment. Caillebotte too was attracted by the magic of the engine, of this totally new environment with its bustling life, as was Manet, who painted the bridge overlooking the railway network.

Monet opted for a completely different vantage point from that chosen by his colleagues. No longer taking a high-angle point of view, nor favoring an external event (a woman and child in Manet's canvas, Place de l'Europe abandoned to the rain in Caillebotte's), Monet showed the bold perspective of the parallel rails, and the trains appear like fantastical, mythological beasts, vibrating with contained energy, belching forth clouds of vapor that enveloped them and brought life to the enormous iron and steel vault of the roof.

From the start, Monet captured the majesty and modernity of the place, its architectural stasis and at the same time the intensity of the life that went on around it.

Though it had moved the spirits and captured the imaginations of poets, never before had this modernity and the vitality of machinery been so vividly portrayed. For Zola, it represented the heartbeat of a completely new society of which he became the bard, the herald, the analyst and conscience.

The Gare Saint-Lazare was at the heart of the European Quarter, so-called because the names of the streets making up its fabric were those of the great European capitals. In this sense, it was the embodiment of that spirit of wandering that inspired all the generations to come.

Anticipating even the rigorously rhymed verse of Blaise Cendrars, which pulsed to a rhythm of machinery, and Valery Larbaud's sensual variations on the grand theme of departures, Claude Monet translated into pictorial terms the impending departure,

67

The Gare Saint-Lazare, Arriving Train. 1877.
Cambridge (Mass.), Fogg Art Museum.
We are not far from Zola's "human beast."

its imminence. In painting the train at the platform, he did not depict it motionless; he suggested a journey. The question remains, as with Watteau's *Embarkation for Cythère*, whether it was a matter of an arrival or a departure. It matters little, since the moment he chose to depict was that of the end to a journey that he has evoked, but held in check. Sooner, or later, he grasps its essential vitality, materialized in the steam that extends and dissipates, unfolding its sultry voluptuousness in an intermingling of hope and regret. Every journey is a quest motivated by hope and its accomplishment is a test. Monet simultaneously expresses all these sentiments, less contradictory than they might seem at first glance.

He gives the pulse of a dream that comes in the guise of reality, included in the ordinary and passing for banality.

Exoticism is within our grasp. It is enough to pay a little more attention to the facts of reality in order to flush it out. This is all the more important in the development of Monet's art, as he did not return to it; he forged his destiny as a painter beyond this reality, in a timeless zone, whereas here his grounding in time takes the function of testimony. Monet's Gare Saint-Lazare represents an epoch; the one that he experienced boldly yet also without fanaticism. He was a witness as were Renoir, Manet, Degas, and even their common enemies the "stuffed shirt" official artists, but the latter merely scratched at the surface of things, while Monet and his friends went beyond the image, realizing that the full potential of painting lay in the medium itself and in new expressive aims.

Monet had set out even more boldly than the others in this adventure, and his testimony could only gain in importance for this; for all the narrative value they have, at the same time they explore the immense potential of painting, gradually eliminating the function of content in favor of the "container", or vehicle, itself.

At the heart of his times, Monet did not lose sight of his aims. Profound and still unconscious, they may well have prompted his choice of an energy made visible by the steam, a concretization of water's potential. Before exploding – magnificently alone – in his great symphonies of plants and water, he hailed here the epic poetry of water as a driving force, of water tamed for man's purposes.

The Railway Bridge at Argenteuil.
Paris, Musée du Louvre.

Madame Monet Seated on Sofa.
Paris, Musée du Louvre.
The discrete charm of the bourgeoisie.

NEAR VETHEUIL

Vetheuil is located some 60 kilometers from Paris. It is a town of 622 inhabitants, with a doctor and a post office. To get there a train from the Gare Saint-Lazare goes as far as Mantes, and from there it is just another dozen kilometers through pleasantly rolling countryside. The village appears suddenly, nestled on the banks of the Seine which leisurely winds its way through the landscape. Monet settled there with Camille and their two sons, together with the Hoschedé family; all counted, they were a dozen individuals packed into a small house wedged against a cliff overlooking the Seine.

At that time, Monet's financial and familial situations were more complicated than ever.

Ernest Hoschedé was a peculiar businesman who had become infatuated with Monet and collected works by his friends as well. At this time, he was in difficult straits, and his wife Alice and Claude Monet were embarking on a relationship that was to last all their lives.

Camille died following a lengthy and painful illness. Monet's affection for Alice, which may have appeared unseemly when the two households were living under the same roof, now had the excuse that thanks to her, his two sons, Jean and Michel, could have a second mother. Ernest Hoschedé was always away, and his behavior was increasingly erratic. Monet, meeting his responsibilities as the head of a large family, wore himself out traveling between Paris and Vetheuil, in hypothetical search of clients. To the great anger of his friends, he decided not to participate in the fifth Impressionist exhibition, in order to try his luck on the side of the official Salon. They spoke of betrayal.

The publisher Charpentier organized an exhibition held in the headquarters of *La Vie Moderne*. But most of all Monet's meetings with Durand-Ruel (who had resurfaced around this time) helped pull the painter out of the financial slump he had gotten himself into. He left Vetheuil in 1881 and settled in Poissy with Alice Hoschedé, who had no reticence about her relationship with the painter. Their next

Spring in Vetheuil.
A hymn to the tranquillity of light and plants.

Paul Durand-Ruel.

The studio in Giverny.

The second studio in Giverny.

Alice Hoschedé.

move was to Giverny in 1883. Alice remained by Monet's side, and tended to the everyday aspects of their life there.

As in Argenteuil, Monet undertook a systematic approach to his locations in Vetheuil. He painted one by one the banks of the Seine and the nearby hills from various angles and in different formats. He was mapping out his territory rather than studying it in depth. His mobility itself bore witness to his dissatisfaction. It was not until the end of his life that he was able to stand still before the infinite mobility of water.

Unlike the other painters, however, he brought method to his observation of the landscape; he carried out the work of a surveyor who plots out the vantage points that offered the best view of given sites in his territory in their natural light and all their special qualities. He was driven by a need to anthologize, to accumulate, that did not yet have the direction or the pacing that appear in his "series".

A break in events happened in this case to be of a natural order: the winter of 1879-80 was an unusually harsh one.

A succession of snowstorms and freezes iced over the river.

Monet went as many as sixteen times to paint the spectacular break-up of the ice on the Seine.

His way of depicting the patchy ice floes on the water, reveals a composition that anticipated his *Water Lilies*. In this wintry wonderland, Monet's gaze turned even more inwards, to his deepest sensations.

The snowscapes that Monet undertook from time to time (in Louveciennes, Argenteuil, Vetheuil, and later in Norway) invite a strange, calm and somewhat mystical contemplation of silence. In them, everything is concentrated, and shrinking. The sun itself seems to contract, as if frightened by the assault of the cold. But at the same time, nothing is dramatized; in painting the unbridled sea, he let himself get carried away in sweeping, showy

Camille on Her Deathbed. 1870.
Paris, Musée du Louvre.
This work heralds Munch's heavy style of Expressionism.

brushstrokes, while here he maintained a sweet, dreamy tone.

While water is the picture of mobility, snow communicates immobility, though it will soon melt, and though its composition itself, the way it is cast over the ground belies the underlying action of the terrain, the vegetation. The snow does not entirely hide what it blankets. It makes up a rich, yet discrete, trimming, alternating the sombre colors of the terrain with its own whiteness, which however is not entirely candid. It is soiled; the tracks of passing carriages and human presence have already reduced it to slush. It is a pessimistic vision that reveals a latent melancholy. The spectacle of the snow invites introspection, a return to the hazy realms of a dormant self, where childhood also plays its part.

Childhood is profoundly marked by this transformation of the environment and the slow, delicious, almost reluctant descent of water as soft as cotton, a caressing lightness. But snow can also be seen as a messenger of death; it can be described as a shroud and it falls to earth at the moment of the latter's deepest dormancy. Beyond words, which were not his tools, in landscapes which could be mere anecdotal pages marking the different stages of his peregrinations, or simply what was before his eyes, Monet distilled something which strongly resembled a rambling meditation, colored with nostalgia and with death at its heart, shadowy, fleeting and hesitant.

The Carriage.
Paris, Musée du Louvre.

Snow at Argenteuil.
Tokyo, National Museum of Western Art.
A completely inward-looking gaze which speaks of the silence of spaces and life muffled by the elements as if by a shroud.

Claude Monet 75

81

Vetheuil: Winter.
New York, Frick Collection.
The soiled snow.

omontory at Etretat. 1885.
aleigh, North Carolina Museum of Art.
he sun punctuates the painting, as in *Impression: Rising Sun.*

The Boat at Giverny.
Paris, Musée du Louvre.

WANDERINGS

Can one still speak of an Impressionist group in 1880? The exhibition held in Rue des Pyramides 10 was, after all, billed as the "Independent painters".

Monet, Renoir, Sisley and Cézanne did not take part in it. In fact, it presented the works of the Degas clan (Mary Cassat, Forain, Rouart, Rafaelli). The former critical and public hostility had turned into an indifference that was no less cruel. Furthermore, the group's supporters began to take their distance. J.K. Huysmans preferred a painting style full of mystery and sparks of intuition – indeed, anecdotal – while Zola stubbornly persisted in his initial vote for a "naturalist" painting style. The Impressionists' evolution towards a pure painting style could not have pleased him. They had, in his opinion, failed. Conceding that "they are all ahead of their time", he pointed out that "not an artist among them has powerfully and definitively developed the new formula, though they have all contributed something to it, scattered among their works". He concluded with regret that the genius who could accomplish this synthesis had not yet been born. At last, admitting an insufficient knowledge to judge Monet the leader of a new current in painting, he said that the painter's only fault was a tendency to drift away from naturalism, which he praised to the exclusion of all else.

Not only did Monet not participate in this fifth Impressionist exhibition, but he bore a sort of rancor towards the group, comparing it to a small sect, criticizing it for having become a "banal school that has opened its doors to the first dauber who comes along".

He was again absent from the 1881 exhibition, held once more at Nadar's in Boulevard des Capucines 35. Like his old friends Renoir, Sisley and Cézanne, he had set his sights on officialdom, on showing at the Salon.

Driven by a youthful élan, material wants, the need for recognition, the ardor of friendship, a shared chafing at the hostility of the elders, the Impressionist group lost its *raison d'être* with the pass-

age of time. In part this was because some of its constituent artists finally found the public approval that they had sought, or patrons who relieved them of material concerns. And in part, it was because their aesthetic conception itself had evolved.

In Monet's case, the sensory objectivity that he had originally pursued no long satisfied him.

From a keen observation of nature, he moved on to an increasingly bold interpretation that no longer focused solely on the facts of reality, but wove around it a web of associations, correspondences, that went far beyond the original idea of naturalism.

He became, as Gustave Geffroy described him, "an anxious observer of the differences between minutes".

A period of wandering along the coast of Normandy (Fécamp, Etretat), Holland, Belle-lle, the shores of the Mediterranean, the Creuse, led him to reflect on his art, in anticipation of his grand finale at Giverny from 1890-1926, the period of his series and the water lilies, the apotheosis. Back near the sea that was so familiar to him, Monet adopted an approach that heralded a truly new conception of painting.

A witness reported having seen "Claude Monet wrapped in a cloak, the rain streaming over him, as he painted the hurricane, doused by great splashes of salt water. He held two or three canvases between his knees, which at intervals of a few minutes he rotated on the easel. They all framed the same section of a cliff with the raging sea, under different lighting effects, fine infiltrations of light falling through breaks in the clouds as if through cellar windows to illuminate the stormy night on the sea of gold and emerald islets set against with bluish tones like the leading of a stained-glass window. The painter stalked each of these effects, a slave to the coming and going of the light, halting his brush at the close of each of its appearances, setting at his feet the incomplete canvas and stalking the return of a discontinued impression to resume in another work".

It was in this period that he achieved his most

brilliant results, almost expressionist, based on the play of tonal contrasts, with a gestural rhythm that is both frenetic and sweeping.

Tired of travel, at fifty years of age and midway along in a life that was already rich in emotions, events and all sorts of difficulties, Monet took his bearings. He finally settled down. His marriage to Alice Hoschedé in 1892 offered a certain stability to his life. Giverny suited him. Furthermore, his dealings with Durand-Ruel assured him of a fairly comfortable living. The latter was in a better position to support the painter. The after-shocks of the depression of 1870 had finally faded. In addition to a net improvement in business trends, and an economic growth that helped build rapid fortunes, Durand-Ruel had found some new patrons who brought considerable sums of money with them.

In 1891, he presented Monet's *Haystacks*. The first of many "series", the painter had done them according to a principle which was not new to him but which he had never formalized. In fifteen or so canvases (the first of which may have been done in 1889), Monet revisited a subject whose banality could have been a serious handicap to their acceptance by the public. Monet took an enormous risk just at a time when his art, like that of his companions the Impressionists, was beginning to meet with the public's approval.

According to Georges Grappe, Monet's determination to impose this style could well have cost him a triumphant début. "With no weakness, no concessions, the painter returned to the fray, where he risked losing all the ground he had gained against snobbism and indifference. That he never wavered in such circumstances is proof of the nobility of his character".

In an epoch in which the public expected from painting a certain form of transport, when it celebrated the technical feats of the official artists who aimed to stun with their historical subjects and rich embellishments, Monet sought to impose an abrupt realism, with a pictorial quality whose boldness derived from the chromatic effects. It is truth, of striking complexity and harmonious sensuality on every inch of the canvas, already heralding the exquisite flowing lines of Art Nouveau or Tiffany's or Gallé's effects of transparency.

Late Summer Haystacks. 1891.
Paris, Musée du Louvre.
To capture the light of an instant. Direct competition with photography.

A SERIAL PAINTER

Blanche Hoschedé, one of Alice's daughters who shared the painter's domestic setting in Giverny, recalled what led Monet to the subject of the haystacks.

"One morning, very early, intent on his subject, Claude Monet was struck by the reflection of the rays of sunlight on a haystack. In one moment the stubble was flooded with sunlight and appeared completely white; in the next, it seemed to be on fire. For months and months, the painter was absorbed in trying to capture this wonderful spectacle. He brought me with him as he crossed the fields. I pushed a wheelbarrow laden with as many canvases as there were impressions for him to capture".

In one of his letters to Gustave Geffroy, Monet declared, "what I seek: instantaneity and especially the atmosphcrc, thc same light spread over everything, and more than ever, I am repelled by the facile, what can be grasped in single glance. I am increasingly obsessed by this need to express what I feel".

This is a key confession for what it reveals to us about the painter's state of mind, his problems and his full awareness, at the time fundamental, of an aim that was to be the driving force behind his work: to no longer separate the object seen from its environment and from the mass of light revealing it, which, however, also has a life of its own, around the object's edges, and altered by the object itself. Union, confluence, repellency of the mass and the void, opacity and transparence, are qualities which inspired Monet and after him the painting of the neo-Impressionists.

Monet's aim to transmit simultaneously a luminous effect and a keen awareness of the moment went far beyond the simple objectives of Impressionism. He was already proposing the expression of emotion that was to be later taken on more fully by the Symbolists.

The difference lay in Monet's adoption of a fine, atomized brush technique, never enclosing his images in the sinuous lines that Gauguin preached and van Gogh practised, though all their aims were similar.

Moreover, since 1886, the year of the last Impressionist group exhibition (in which Monet did not participate, his last having been that of 1882), the group disbanded, each one of them at grips with his own specific quest. The public no longer ignored them, and especially Monet met with a success that made it possible for him to steer his career in an independent direction that before would have been inconceivable. By no means indifferent to the commercial aspects of his art, Monet was one of the best-selling – and highest paid – painters of the 1880s.

His decorative aims are clearly declared in the Poplar series. Octave Mirbeau complimented the artist on the "absolute beauty of his great decorations". Even more than the Haystacks series, the Poplars made up a homogeneous whole.

It was not so much the design (though here it was more defined) than the rhythms themselves of the series as a whole that bore a similarity to the sinuous lines of Symbolism. In fact, Gustave Geffroy remarked that the painter wished "to represent with flourish the face of the universe, to bring everything together in the pure incandescence of solar illumination".

An obvious linear stylization, undulating and flickering, heralded the "modern" style's drift towards the decorative. Apart from the rhythms which here are precisely calculated to achieve a perfect musicality, the painter paid careful attention to his palette, reaching a truly new height of sensibilities and keen perception.

In spite of this decorative aspect, Monet remained faithful to reality. Indeed, he could not do without it. He had a physical need to have the "motif" that he painted before his eyes. And in fact, when he learned from his buyer that the Poplars series had to be terminated, he struck up a deal with the latter in order to obtain a temporary reprieve for his subject.

More than any other of his series, the Rouen Cathedrals invite comparison with photography. From a single vantage point (a window of a building almost facing the Cathedral), Monet made a composite of "snapshots" that the eye alone could not combine, the whole of it embraced by the momentary vision.

The imposing, yet slender, mass of the cathedral is in some way sculpted by the light that gives life to the architectural relief. He did not paint with the idea of rivaling photography, even though its techniques interested him and helped him to understand better the problems surrounding the depiction of reality. His idea was to capture as accurately as possible a phenomenon that was at the heart of his latest work. He only wished to be true and precise, and this was prophetic. Painting no longer represented a reality fixed forever in a false eternity, but embraced the intangible expression of our life, which can only be truly represented in movement. One can follow from canvas to canvas the revolving movement of the light. At the two extremes, that is at the break of dawn and at dusk, the imagination replaces observation, as if the last steps were so dizzying that the sublime moment of transition between lightness and obscurity was in fact truly impossible to capture. Thus, Monet presented us with cathedrals having the fascination of phantoms.

Lastly, unlike the themes of the haystacks and the poplars, where he had the subject close before him, with the cathedrals it was materially impossible to paint them on the site itself. He was thus led to adopt an approach which was not at all at odds with his drive for realism, but which enhanced the role of memory in his painting.

With the series of the *Mornings on the Seine,* started in 1896-97, Monet played more openly with a sort of stylization that anticipated Symbolism. At the point where the Epte river flows into the Seine, quite close to Giverny, Monet went on pre-dawn forays to capture the highly subtle and transitory effect of the mist filtering the light of the rising sun. In several paintings, the delicate vibrancy of colors

Poplars Along the Epte River.
London, Tate Gallery.

Yellow Iris.
London, Marlborough Gallery.

Woman Reading.
Private collection.

95

blending one into the other renders precisely the immateriality of the subject. But in his choice of palette (mauve, pink, green, purple, pale blue) he responded to the aesthetic aspirations of Mallarmé, "who sought to endow the facts described with as many shades of meaning as possible", as Joël Isaacson pointed out, adding the acute observation that these immaterial *Mornings* were quite in harmony with the fin-de-siècle atmosphere: "They also bring Proust to mind, with his search for the echoes – faint but still there – of the past".

The Portal (Sun).
New York, Metropolitan Museum of Art.
The phantasmic architecture at the threshold hour when daylight cedes
to nightfall.

Morning on the Seine near Giverny. 1897.
New York, Metropolitan Museum of Art.

The Seine near Vetheuil.
Rotterdam, Museum Boymans.
The water, sky and plant-life treated as pictorial materials and not as
anecdotes.

LONDON AND VENICE

London and Venice: sister cities for their indecisive light that plays over an extraordinary range of hues, from the finest and most transparent to the most opaque. In 1889, Monet was finally able to return to London, no longer in exile as in 1871, but in quest of a new subject. He settled at the Hotel Savoy, where he had a sweeping view of the Thames. He painted the bridge of Waterloo, that of Charing Cross and that of Westminster, as well as the dramatic silhouette of the Parliament building, with its sharp pinnacles and stone crenelations, which was well-suited to the type of phantasmagorical visions that Monet turned to now. Tired of the mist, or emerging from it, he gave us the dreamy settings for the kind of Gothic novels of complex intrigue that were so popular in France at the start of the century. Oddly, Monet made the transition between this Gothic literature and the "Nabist" movement, and though he was more concerned with synthesis, he was also open to eerie atmospheres.

Never content with just one view, in the course of several visits (in 1900 and 1901) Monet unflaggingly took up the same motifs over and over.

Durand-Ruel's exhibition of these works had to wait until 1904 because, as the artist himself confessed, he had painstakingly labored on the canvases in the studio and "because for the work I do, it is essential for me to have them all before my eyes, and to tell the truth, not a single one of them is definitively finished. I manage them as a whole". Even more than the other series, this one represented a compact whole. Thirty-seven canvases made up the series of the views of London and the Thames, forming a coherent set that in effect lost in value if seen separately. Octave Mirbeau, who organized the exhibition, recalled that it showed "four years of reflective observation, of determined efforts, and prodigious work". The critic Charles Morice spoke of "the dark and smoky capital of another world".

"How unfortunate that I did not come here when

The Westminster Bridge.
Private collection.

Monet in St. Mark's Square, Venice.

Dusk in Venice.
National Gallery of Wales.
The subtlety of the "modern style."

I was younger and more daring", wrote Monet upon his arrival in Venice in 1908. He found there another version of that shifting light that fired his imagination. In painting the famous monuments of the city, he emptied them of all their anecdotal and picturesque charge, retaining just their appearance, with the complex reflection of light from the water playing over their somewhat magnified shapes.

Alice's death in 1911 overwhelmed him with profound grief, barring him from a return to these places as he had planned in order to check his paintings against their models, as he had done with the London series. At the same time, he was dissatisfied with the series and practically abandoned it, declaring on the occasion of its unveiling at the Bernheim-Jeune gallery (in 1912), "It is dreadful. I went to Venice twice with my wife. I took some notes and planned to return. But my wife died and I did not have the heart to go. So I finished it from memory. Nature has taken its revenge". This is not just a bitter reflection, but rather a statement of the artist's respect of nature, whose unique quality he felt he must render, even if in the studio. He let himself go with the flow of his imagination, changing, enriching the work, endowing it with a personal and poetic dimension that would resonate over time.

THE FREEDOM TO BE

The Impressionist group was founded for the simple reason of strength in number, and in fact, many of the participants in the first exhibition were soon forgotten mediocre artists. Rather than representing a unified approach, a shared philosophy or a common aesthetic, they were the mouthpiece for the new – and very radical – idea of the artist's freedom to be. The 19th century hastened the decline of ideologies adopted in the 18th century regarding the development of a society founded on equality and fraternity. Liberty remained: it was the last truth allowed, and it was frenetically experienced. After all, it was precisely the 19th century that gave rise to the most categorical, solitary adventures, the most removed from any concept of the school or the group. Society itself had abandoned the idea of a cogent aesthetic through which it could express itself or find a self-identity. To the degree that the 17th century was the incarnation of an all-powerful monarchy, transmitter of cultural forces, the 19th century was the gauge of the widening gap that had appeared between political power and creativity.

For lack of a collective spirit (which had become impossible) individual initiative was taken to an extreme, and became a sort of criteria for quality. The realm of scientific realism entailed the rise of intellectual relativism, offering to each man his own personal truth and the right to experience it to its farthest limits.

Thus, the inevitable divorce between the creator and society was set in motion: the latter could no longer identify in the former that element of collective truth that until then he had represented.

Ideology stood unsteadily on its foundations and this contributed to the launch of unique phenomena, which represented rejection taken to an extreme.

Without going as far as the categorical break with society experienced by van Gogh and Gauguin, Monet was involved in such a personal pursuit that it eluded the understanding of his contemporaries,

Break-up of Ice on the Seine.
Liverpool, Walker Art Gallery.
An anticipation of the trailing brushstrokes of the water lilies.

apart from a few more perceptive observers. And his success did not necessarily mean that the public had understood what he wished to express; more often they saw in his work only what they wished to see in it.

Not only did Monet no longer paint a compact, easily recognizable and reassuring world, but he also undertook a sort of somnambular wandering through atomized, imprecise shapes fragmented in the light to the point of losing their substance. Faithful to the real because he stood before it to paint, he ended up by showing only its intangible side, the fleeting, the fluid, the unprecedented magic of its very inaccessibility. While others painted affirmations, certainties, he painted true-to-life uncertainties. While van Gogh was in the grips of a regression, heaving with invectives, and ending with an inevitable suicide, Monet was involved in a sort of long slide into the heart of the visible, on a watery path where the spirit dissolved in a pantheism that annihilated man in favor of a totality without frontiers, which no image could truly contain. Monet took painting to its extreme limits, by emphasizing these limits themselves, the fundamental incompatibility between its definition and what this must embrace.

A NEW STYLE OF PAINTING

Reduced to what the human body could express, concentrated, channeled into its anatomy, all of life's energy powered the athletes plucked by Michelangelo from their miserable hovels so he could make gods of them.

He transcended man by the beauty of man. After all, the Renaissance had constructed the world around man endowed with his full powers.

While Rubens headed off this notion of an all-powerful, dominating humanism, he let a new feeling quicken in his work: disquiet.

His athletes acquired a mood of anxiety which soon eroded the sureness that they had formerly possessed. Romanticism was not far in the offing and soon plunged painting into tumult. The fusion of man and space took place in a key of tragedy.

At the same time, the artist no longer concentrated on man as master of the world, but rather on this world, which he discovered to be much more diverse than he had been led to believe, with many areas of shadow, of the unknown left to explore, enormous virgin territories. All told, the questions far outnumbered the answers.

Romanticism replaced pride with fire, grandeur with anxiety, certainties with doubt.

Delacroix took on a painting style of protest and transformed it into a painting style that vibrated, whose only *raison d'être* lay in the action itself of painting.

From this emerged the importance of the brushstroke, up to then restrained, dominated, synonymous with bad taste.

Monet came onto the scene at this point, where painting was shifting dangerously toward its own materiality. But it was the hour of the objectivity of science. If God was dead, reason reigned supreme. It was absolute reality that answered his investigations.

New laws of physics were discovered; it was now better understood and admitted that life's energy was not just concentrated on man, but it was pervasive and that it made up just one part of a vast plan of creation.

113

There was awareness of the importance of understanding and analyzing the shifting equilibrium between man and his natural environment.

But before following the lead of the scientists – who from then on would be the true poets – Monet had learned from painters who studied the objective facts of nature. With the passing of time, this seemed to be, paradoxically, a regression of art. But the Barbizon school, which worked towards an alliance with nature, with everyday reality, had prepared the ground for a collapse of the traditional values of representation.

In depicting what he saw, the painter came up against the inconsistencies of sight; he discovered his own shortcomings and suffered the obsoleteness of his techniques.

Monet sooner than the others, perhaps because his drive had gotten stronger and rebelled against naturalism as well as academicism. He could not be satisfied with an objectivity that admitted to its own shortcomings.

The fact was that the truth in painting lay elsewhere.

HOW DOES YOUR GARDEN GROW

Monet's love for the garden was a constant factor in his life, and one that grew until it was his sole source of inspiration. In each place where he settled – in Ville d'Avray, Louveciennes, Argenteuil and Vetheuil – he left convincing proof of this.

Of course, in each of these cases, his gardens were mere settings, but they had a luxuriance, a refinement, an abundance, a sensuality that was striking. And there, his study of the plant world was only supplemental to a more general vision in which objects and people also played a part. But he demonstrated a particular sensibility to natural things, a special care in depicting their existence, a keen awareness of their vivacity. Doubtlessly because his gaze was not trained for cultural references, but rather for a direct contact with nature, Monet perceived the plant world in his own personal way.

A child of the sea, used to its vast spaces and the manifestations of the elements, he did not see the plant world as an added decoration, but as an entity that took on increasing importance, to the point that in his final period, it dispelled all other realities. A lifelong gardener, at Giverny he adopted an almost scientific method, described by J.P. Hoschedé.

At Giverny, Monet had found a large orchard extending before the house with two long flowerbeds on each side of a central path, planted with ranks of spruce and cypress trees between them and edged with boxwood hedges. Monet added a flowered vault made of metal arches covered with rambling roses, its gravel path planted with creeping nasturtiums that grew in "graceful sinuous patterns", forming a richly colored carpet.

Enlarging his garden, Monet tirelessly modified it: "the west side became a well-kept lawn, abundantly watered and regularly manicured. On this great lawn, Monet planted here and there clusters of irises and oriental poppies. Fruit trees which had died or been uprooted were replaced with flowering trees, such as ornamental cherry and apple trees, but not as densely as before.

The side was laid out in successive 'banks', each

Monet's Garden at Giverny.
The universe reduced to a garden was enough for the painter to express himself and to set in motion painting's adventure in modernity.

decorated with various plant species. Gladiolas, larkspur, phlox, asters, large daisies. [...] Almost all the garden's flowerbeds had wide borders of all types of plants, whatever Monet had a particular fondness for. Each year, the number of species introduced to the garden increased, with a highly colorful effect. These plants were usually of the perennial type, with simple flowers. Nevertheless, annuals were scattered among the perennials so that there were always flowers in bloom and also very little earth showed through the dense greenery".

Stressing Monet's meticulous nature as a gardener, Hoschedé went on to explain that "Monet was well-informed about gardening, having consulted all the horticultural journals and catalogues and visited the gardens of others, in particular that of Georges Truffaut".

He organized his flowerbeds like pictorial compositions, distributing the flowers as if from a palette. "He knew what he wished to obtain from the plants that he had gotten and had planted in such and such a place, not at random, but with the certainty of the effect they would produce. He knew well in advance that when they would be in full bloom, their size and color would be in perfect harmony with those adjacent to them and the over-all effect of the garden".

With his creation of the water lily pond, he brought a piece of the Orient to the Norman climate.

He made this aquatic garden from scratch. Starting with a bit of meadow, he created "the most beautiful of landscapes because he had put in some water so that the sky could be reflected in it, along with the plants, some afloat, – the red, pink, yellow and white water lilies – and others, such as irises, to mark the curve of the banks, the whole creating a delight for the eyes. A thicket of roses hugged by rhododendrons, azaleas and hydrangeas marked the property's edges, and then an arched bridge in the Japanese style overhung with white and mauve wisteria spanned the pond. [...] On the narrow lawn bordering the pond, there were tree peonies with large and simple red, pink and garnet-colored flowers. All of this was dominated by the trees, willows and poplars".

Proud of his garden, Monet often repeated to his guests that "My finest masterpiece is my garden".

Monet in driving togs.

A STUDIO BIOGRAPHY

Too heavily steeped in legend and the hunger for the picturesque, the history of painting in the 19th century dressed the artists' biographies to the measure of an almost unhealthy curiosity: for pain, for example, as if by acknowledging it, it could be set right, just as today, paradoxically, van Gogh's inferno of solitude attracts pressing crowds to exhibitions of his work. An uneventful life could be made interesting in the hands of the panegyrists, historians in search of the smallest crumb that could enrich and make picturesque a painter's life. However, instead of drawing a lifelike profile, they carved out a caricature. A life lived with intensity does not necessarily mean accents, a colorful character, attention-grabbing events. Indeed, these can sometimes eclipse the essential.

The generation of artists that made up the Impressionist group and other related currents in art (since that period, art has evolved according to a very simple sort of dialectic) did not escape this dramatization of their lives. Unlike the artists of the past – who faded into anonymity as servants of the court, the church or the craft guilds – 19th-century artists had to live out their existence as artists proper in a society that no longer called on them for their services, and in the name of a marginality that the artists embraced, sometimes quite proud about it and sometimes at the cost of putting more art into their lives than into their work.

Claude Monet's life seen in this new perspective shows neither an unbridled individualism nor an anonymity devoid of anecdotal situations. He let the meaning of his life slide imperceptibly into his work, giving it a life of its own, just the essence of life.

Claude Monet's life, including the hard times, joys, risks and phases of his development, does not entirely explain his work, though it does offer some illumination. Monet had none of Degas' misanthropy, Cézanne's brutish unsociability, van Gogh's self-destructive preoccupation with the sordid aspects of life, nor did he have Manet's hunger for

The Monet family.

Monet family on a picnic.

The Giverny dining room.

Jean astride his hobby horse.

worldliness that led the latter to compromise himself at times, on the side of the official artists, their common enemy.

Claude Monet, born into a petit-bourgeois family, remained a man of that class, that environment, fond of simple comforts, committed to a regular and above all hardworking lifestyle: little adventure, a family man in his sentiments, a few steady friendships with men of his rank and culture.

In Giverny during the last phase of his long life, Monet seemed to be at the peak of this serenity, and this permitted him to devote himself entirely to his work, even though at the end he suffered greatly over the death of his wife Alice Hoschedé – with whom he had lived a perfect family life surrounded by many children – and grave problems with his sight.

Jean-Pierre Hoschedé, a precious witness to this intimate life, described some of its most significant aspects.

"The family was made up of eight children, big and small, often filled out by a few cousins, and later by some grandchildren. All this made for a lot of noise, cries and laughter, but far from getting angry, Monet often took part in our games".

There were endless tennis and croquet matches, and Monet showed a predilection for the cup-and-bowl game.

"At home, after dinner on Sundays and Thursdays we got together over a game of cards, playing for low stakes. But the game that Monet preferred to all others was checkers. He was very good at it. [...] In his old age, when he was alone, he developed a liking for backgammon.

"Monet liked to read in the evenings, especially during the winter. He preferred reading out loud. His literary taste ranged broadly. His favorite authors were the Goncourts, Octave Mirbeau, Flaubert, Gustave Geffroy, Zola, Tolstoy, Jules Renard, Ibsen, Clemenceau, Maëterlinck, Lucien Descaves".

He made the most of his garden, enjoying the cool evenings there, and he liked to go mushroom hunting and canoeing.

"Monet was not a gourmand, but he was a gourmet, and he had a very good appetite. When he was in a good mood – which was not always the case, given the setbacks he suffered due to the effects of the weather on his subjects – he would break into song as he sat down at the table, crying out and singing to the tune of Carmen's Toreador: 'A table, à table, à table mangeons ce pigeonneau qui ne saurait être bon s'il n'était mangé chaud'."

Monet loved good wine and simple dishes. He was a fussy eater, and often liked to prepare his own meals.

The whole family loved to go on trips and the car was a highly appreciated family acquisition.

It was inevitable that Monet at times should fall victim to heavy bouts of discouragement, noted also by his family. Despite the extraordinary speed with which he turned out his paintings, the work was draining, and he was shaken by doubts which were sometimes difficult to overcome.

"Sometimes he took things out on the canvas, violently, as if to punish himself. Afterwards sulky and a little bit ashamed of himself, he would then go off to bed and we would not see him for a day or two".

It was a family chronicle rich in detail and striking for its similarity to that of any bourgeois family of the period. Monet managed to keep the equilibrium between his work as a painter and his private life; either his sense of decency or his wisdom kept him from sacrificing one for the other.

AN ABSOLUTE PRESENT

Nature's growing role in art over time can be seen as a very long zoom shot starting with a distant vision and gradually passing to such a close-up view that it penetrated to nature's most private parts, to the heart of its energies. The primitives set the landscape in the distance, and their discourse essentially stemmed from the scene that they depicted. Thus nature's role was little more than that of scenery and its frontal perspective was similar to what is painted on theatrical backdrops.

Gradually, painters tightened the perspective of the landscape, until it became the subject of the painting. This took a few centuries and a progressive loosening of the bonds between the artist and his patron. The painter at the service of power, whose task it was to celebrate the latter's grandeur, would have had a hard time indeed devoting himself, without betraying his patron, to the vision of nature.

It was through a series of subterfuges that painters succeeded in assigning a place of importance to nature. The 18th century was a sort of parenthesis that favored this naturalist celebration, because it was the fashion. But the onslaught of classicism eclipsed it again, focusing on man in action. It was with naturalism and the new independent role of the painter in society that nature found new favor. Since the painter no longer had to pander to the vanity of a patron, he could turn to the facts of ordinary life, and pick up the threads of a buried instinct.

A painting embraces a present that has been pared down to the thousandth of a second, even though the painter may have worked at length to achieve his effect of illusion. Painting aspired to perfection, but it could never be anything but illusion. "Trompe l'oeil" is how these paintings are described – so accurately do they depict their subject that you could reach out to touch it. And when you touch the surface of the canvas it is surprising to discover that your eye has deceived you!

Painting crystallizes an eternal present hurled headlong toward a future that engulfs it and drags it toward its destruction. The future is the enemy of

Water Lilies, Left Side.
Paris, Orangerie.

Water Lilies.
Private collection.

Water Lilies, Right Side.
Paris, Orangerie.

Water Lilies.
Zurich, Fondation Bührle.

the present. Painting, which is just an image, never depicts more than a present that is already part of the past. At best, it transforms an endangered present into an idealized past. It also serves as a vehicle for much nostalgia.

Today, art overloaded with narrative detail enjoys an immense success, as does art that settles on aspects of nature that are obsolete, held at an arm's length that is explicitly declared in the work. Like photography, it fuels nostalgia, using identical means, those of narrative.

Monet's later work totally sidesteps this phenomenon, because it does not depict an endangered present but rather a perpetual present: nature at its energy-giving origins. The ability to render tangible what underlies life, to follow the drives of the great body of the universe itself, is what saves his painting from this transitoriness and from the indelible marks of its own time.

The *Water Lilies* are less modern than they are timeless. They only seem modern to us because they are in keeping with a way of perceiving the universe that they foreshadowed, according to a method that they established and which today an entire pictorial current has adopted, taking them as models.

The water lily pond from another angle.

A STORY OF WATER

At the earth's beginning, in the instant that it left its unformed state and started to take shape, there was water. The mother of all energy. Permanent force, which then became wed with light. Monet was the witness: a magnificent observer of ageless phenomena which sweep along with them the essence of all mythology. In this rising against the current, passing from the imagery of his time made trite by anecdote, all the way to the creative source of all things, Claude Monet completed a course never attempted by any other painter. He was unique in this quest.

For him, painting was not an act of representation. He did not raise with the strokes of his brush a theater curtain – this he left to the others. The carousel of human life did not interest him. For him, painting was an act of celebration. Thus his painting should be read not as an image but as an act. Each stroke, each impact, each flowing touch, each vibration, has a value in itself as such, for its form and its rhythm.

The more deeply involved he got in this adventure, the more he upset notions that up to then had been respected. From 1890 to 1926, he reversed a number of trends in painting, the focus of which by then had shifted from the act to representation, and from the creative impulse to simple craftsmanship.

That he reduced his repertoire of subjects to the pond at Giverny had a significance: its light and water were enough inspiration for him. There, all the phenomena that give order and life to the world took place.

At the heart of an exciting, ephemeral world, shifting and elusive in its totality, Monet "took the plunge" into the chasm of space and time. That he selected water as his subject shows that he was well aware of his mission, even if he never explained it, nor attempted to justify it with theories. That was too far from his style. For him, the act was everything. It suffices to see how the pictorial technique of the *Water Lilies* introduces the idea of a search. The pictorial gesture is so obvious, declared and

The Seine at Giverny. 1885.
Paris, Musée Marmottan
The start of Expressionism lies in this uneven, nervous, angry, savage
stroke which extracts expression from space.

Monet in a typical pose.

even privileged, that the viewer's gaze is drawn to it, at the expense of the overall image. The impression prevails so heavily over the representation and the expression is so spontaneous that the gaze, as it seeks to grasp the whole, gets entangled in the paint itself.

Physical immobility is paired with the awakening of the consciousness. One traces the path of the warm signs of life in the water, as we do in life: an instant transfixed before this slow movement of algae, this calm and apparent mobility gives an awareness of time passing that transforms the water into the living tissue of nature. It is significant that, having tried to express the passage of time through a succession of images, with fixed layouts, using photography as his model, Monet passed to this animation in a single place: the Giverny pond. He preferred the cinematographic idiom to that of photography. His hand, in this comparable to the camera, swept across the field of vision, guiding the gaze as forms unfolded in space.

River's Edge. 1856.
Paris, Musée Marmottan.
An early attempt which already shows a remarkable sensitivity.

A FERTILE EYE

As he made rapid progress in the refinement of his art and he daringly penetrated to the heart of natural phenomena, Monet postured himself neither as a thinker, nor, all the more to reason, as a moralist. Rather, he avoided a painting style that claimed this sort of aim and that pretended to visualize concepts or an intellectual tone. For him, painting was above all a question of sight. It would become an "expression", but as such it was not a confession, the exacerbation of a self transcended by a keen new awareness of its identity.

Though he identified himself with the nature that he painted, Monet did not add that dimension that today arouses excessive interest: psychoanalysis.

For him, everything was limited to the eye, and he was content to simply observe. It was the task of the painter's hand to transcribe what he saw.

While Monet's eye was not intellectual, it was particularly sensitive to the subtlest physical nuances, especially where light was concerned. He risked straying into more – or less – personal considerations of the ephemeral, of passing time, and lapsing into the nostalgic, which is what others did, paradoxically with a static painting style.

Instead, he quite simply placed himself between the viewer's gaze and shifting nature. He presented his paintings as the results of an eye capable of freezing a visual effect to the thousandth of a second. In short, he presented himself as an artist who had discovered a painting technique that could meet the challenges of photography.

The nostalgia that today his paintings seem to convey is added by the viewer who adopts the same attitude before one of Monet's paintings as before a sepia-colored photograph offering the remnants of a deeply buried past.

Perspective. While he penetrated reality, he ferreted about in this extraordinary subject, adventuring into realms until then unexplored. No doubt he very quickly understood that there was nothing to invent here, or rather that everything had already been invented. He noticed that there was no

choice but to follow in the footsteps of others. Not that he had the cultural preparation to back this idea up – to the contrary, but he knew instinctively that he had entered on the tail-end of a discourse in which everything had already been said, only superficially. For lack of invention, he went further into the déjà vu.

He hit upon two new ideas that as of yet had not been explored by painting: the expression of time (the "series") and the expression of space as an entity (the *Water Lilies*).

To express space, he painted a canvas without an end, a sort of "work in progress"; and to express time he worked on the same motif, painting it at different moments, passing from the instantaneity of photography to the simultaneity of cinematography.

In the same way that Marcel Proust's sentences became fragmented in the expression of the sensation, of the impression received and experienced, Monet's painting was fragmentary. The approach of the series emphasizes the idea of groping one's way

Monet standing by the water lily pond.

through time and entering into a drift toward the imaginary.

It is not the least of the paradoxes inherent in his painting style that he came close to the realm of the fantastic while seeking only pure realism.

No doubt this is because the fantastic is reality from a distorted perspective. If it does not refer to the "known" it loses all effect. The fantastic is also born of a simple correction of normal, everyday sights. A simple mist suspended over a landscape, modifying its general lines, distills new values from it, taking the most banal reality toward a world of pure phantasmagoria. Monet also strayed, if only for his tendency to use more and more allusion in his painting, toward these twilight realms that encourage reverie. Thus, it was, in effect, a dreamed reality.

The abandonment of old pictorial formulae that distilled distinct images in space and organized objects as if they were trapped in a theatrical perspective, led Monet to a radical dissolution of figures, where the relationship of figure to background disappeared. And with it, the tragedy of the representation of ancient mythology, for example. Man was no longer set in the presence of divinities that he had invented to frighten himself and that he worshiped to reassure himself; rather, he confronted natural phenomena that gave him a new idea of himself and that encouraged him to reconsider his role in the world – he was no longer the product of a culture, but an integral part of the whole. Monet's radical novelty consisted in no longer painting as an escape or a diversion, but to the contrary, as a way to find himself.

Cézanne. *The Arc Valley.*
Private collection.

THE RETURN TO DEPTH

To paint the awareness of oneself in the bosom of nature: no one had ever attempted a similar objective prior to Monet. Nature had been a setting, or even better, a frame, held in check in order to highlight a moral idea, an intellectual value, a concept. It is meaningful that Cézanne, taking Poussin as his reference, completely distorted the latter's lesson by taking the setting selected by the author of the *Seasons* and pushing it toward a geometrical organization that cancelled the details, resulting in a hierarchy of layers of elements like a puzzle, where nothing could be subtracted for fear of ruining the image.

It was a construction closed to the point of petrification, paving the way for Cubism, which also sought to demonstrate the organization of a constructed world.

Despite appearances, Cézanne was quite close to Monet in terms of method, though they diverged widely in terms of style. Where Cézanne constructed filled-in images, Monet marked out the void.

They were at opposite poles of the same system, based on a new way to view reality which focused on its molecular composition and its living texture instead of anecdotal details.

Cézanne moved in the direction of the eternal, Monet in the direction of the ephemeral.

In painting a world that was imperishable, Cézanne abstracted the energy of its timelessness, its invulnerability. It is significant that he turned to a mineral landscape, erected against an unchanging serene sky, framed by the most resistant types of vegetation, evergreens. Quite to the contrary, Monet was drawn to the fluidity of air and water. While Monet created an art based wholly on the impression, Cézanne worked on certainties.

This extraordinary antagonism between the two extremes of a single system finds confirmation in the respective heritages of the two artists.

Cézanne, through Cubism, gave birth to geo-

metric abstraction, the definition of a perfect world; Monet introduced the notion of motion to painting, which was continued and developed in action paint- ing, the informal and lyrical abstraction, all differ- ent ways of expressing mood, which is the im- pression taken to its extreme.

A FATHER OF EXPRESSIONISM

Since 1908, Monet had complained of sight problems, and in 1912 a double cataract was diagnosed. The progressive deterioration of his sight intensified his problems as a painter and significantly altered his style.

Thiebault-Sissons noted that the artist could no longer see the details of color and shape as well, but, as Joël Jackson remarked, "his perception of the relationships between colors and the atmosphere remained intact, and he experienced greater sensitivity to the more intense shades of color. His altered sight, nevertheless, suited the large dimensions of the canvases he was working on, and his brushstroke broadened as a result".

Just as he broadened and intensified his brushstrokes, he brightened his palette. He applied his paints more thickly, and found in their substance a way of depicting the luxuriant growth of plants, their development in space. "The canvases of 1923 and 1925 reach an intensity of color, clashing reds, greens, oranges and yellows that convey the impression of a brutal response – though still ecstatic – to despair, and at the same time to the painter's raised hopes when he partially recovered his sight". Back then, and quite rightly, an almost expressionist technique was spoken of. Would it be correct then, to identify him as one of the forefathers of this movement, which is usually traced to the very singular, uneven style of van Gogh?

Any possible connection drawn between the Expressionists and this stage in Monet's development disappears when the question of content is raised. The raw material of the Expressionist's anger is nowhere to be found in Monet. While he shows a tendency to expand his subjectivity, to blow it up to the point of its dissolution in the universe, with a sort of global confusion between the meaning and the visible in the act of painting itself, in the Japanese style, Monet never relied on the specific sensation; he did not localize it. This was specifically the realm of the Expressionists.

Rather, he went beyond it, he transcended it,

The Japanese Bridge
Minneapolis, Institute of Art.
The paints themselves burn with an inward fire.

Monet following his cataract operation.

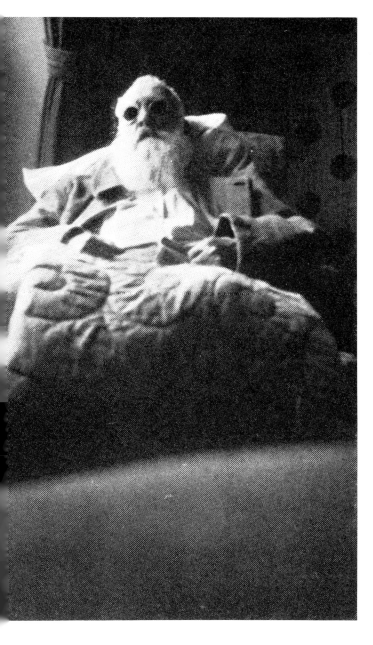

while the Expressionists kept a firm grip on the impression and its quality of elusiveness. On the other hand, something in Monet's handling heralds Expressionism – a roughness of touch, the thickly applied paints that burst into flame and melt, burning with an almost unbearable ardor.

André Masson noted that "in any case, streaked or swept with spirals or wild tangles of lines, the violence of these brushstrokes at one time impaired a scandalized public from 'seeing the landscape'. Take some distance, they told him. Today this advice has been reversed: get closer, and touch with your eyes the most stunning proof of the whirlwind that kindles painterly instinct". In short, Monet was reproached for having painted the ardor, the passion, the fire that consumes the soul, and sears the eye that perceives it.

MONET TO DATE

Painting had become language at its source and no longer one of repertoire; it represented a quest, no longer certainties, identification not description, expression, not necessarily communication.

It sought to transmit, to share, an impression – even if ordinary – with anyone, without the intermediary of a code. Breaking all rules, canons and conventions that had conditioned it, starting with Monet, painting became freedom of self-expression conquered, acquired at great cost, at the sacrifice of official recognition, medals, even the opportunity to decorate public buildings. Could the Monet of the *Water Lilies* have been entrusted with a wall of the city hall, a Chamber of Commerce ceiling or the halls of a Senate building?

And even if he had been, he would not have played according to the rules imposed by such a commission: to offer a decoration that could be understood by all, that is, to fall under the yoke of academicism, which Monet and his companions so abhorred.

Isolated by the grandeur of his aims, the folly of his dreams, the egocentrism of his "style", Claude Monet could not be of any use to society. His language was not civic-minded – though thanks to the evolution of public taste and understanding, it became identified with that of the "tribe" described by Rimbaud.

This "tribe" meant a group of individuals united by a single cause, rallied under a single banner. In Monet's case, this meant a new style of painting projected toward the future.

What he painted in 1925 was gradually, but ever-so-slowly, accepted as the maturing of a new gaze on reality, one that no longer touched upon its surface but penetrated to its most intimate fluctuations, its most imperceptible flutterings, its radiant vitality, with the most exquisite nuances at the same time vertiginous.

Painting for Monet was a solitary act, but his canvas became polyvalent, a mirror in which little by little all those who, like him, yearned for a new relationship with the world could recognize themselves.

While Monet rejected all demagoguery, he did not reject exemplarity. It is the tragedy of all those who are ahead of their time that to become an example takes time. It is logical that Monet should have kindled Surrealism, which passing through Masson channeled this generous creative flow into the canvas, according to a principle of gestuality that he advocated and applied. Invented.

His was a flowing wandering line that depicted not so much the visible as the perceptible; it was something that did not yet have a name, but which was to become Jackson Pollock's "dripping", and J.P. Riopelle's chromatic intensity with that aura of transport charging the space with energy, rather than simply filling it. This "major contemporary", as J.D. Rey put it so well, invented the "film version" of painting, in the sense that it takes form before our very eyes, while previously it was done in the secrecy of the studio, shielded from our gaze and fixed in the images produced.

Style can be identified in the unity of a lifework, not the effect of an instant. A great deal of patience is required as knowledge is acquired, built up, coordinated and synthesized into a coherent formula.

Monet's style did not emerge until his later works. It stands to reason that these were based on earlier works and would never have been possible without the groping progress made with the first, paring down, enriching, correcting, refining, discovering, venturing at risk in and around visible forms, broaching on realms of uncertainty, the undefinable, the intangible, the relative, the changing.

Like all artists of his time, Monet was at grips with a totally new problem that had taken on urgency with the spread of photography: that of movement.

The impossibility of fixing movement on canvas led some painters to turn their backs on it. Cézanne, for example, crystallized his style, culminating in the monolithic near-geometry of his still lifes, the image of immobility, the lasting, timeless. Degas insisted on a style of representation that relied on the figure (the woman at her toilette, or the horse) and gradually replaced realistic forms with that flash of lines and colors that merged in a single spirit – less movement made visible than a displacement of space that annihilates form.

Later artists pursued movement according to techniques directly borrowed from the photographic process. At this stage, the shortcomings of painting in this respect were made clearly evident. But, while it is not suited to depicting real movement, painting could express the movement of the act (of painting) itself; it could make visible the creative spasm that is dictated more by emotion than by a physical law. Monet in this sense foreshadowed all contemporary trends by freeing himself of the aim of realistic representation to pursue the exhilaration of the act of painting.

1840	*Paris. November 14, Rue Lafitte. Claude Monet is born, son of a well-to-do grocer.* Rodin and Odilon Redon are born in the same year. Cézanne and Sisley are both one year old.
1841	Bazille, Renoir and Berthe Morisot are born.
1845	*The Monet family settles in Le Havre. Claude discovers the sea.* The mechanical loom is invented. Schumann: *Piano Concerto*. Wagner: *Tannhäuser*. Mérimée: *Carmen*.
1846	Invention of the rotary printing press. Fromentin is in Algeria. Berlioz: *La Damnation de Faust*. Georges Sand: *La Mare au diable*.
1847	Marx and Engels: *The Communist Manifesto* (published in German). Couture: *Les Romains de la Décadence*. Millet: *La Baratteuse*. Wiertz: *La Belle Rosine*. Emily Brontë: *Wuthering Heights*. Thackeray: *Vanity Fair*. Death of Mendelssohn.
1848	Revolutions in the Austro-Hungarian Empire, Italy and France. Founding of the Second Republic. Formation of the pre-Raphaelite group in England. First experiments with concrete in building construction. Liszt is in Weimar, starting his *Symphonic Poems*. Wagner: *Lohengrin*. Renan: *L'Avenir de la Science*. Death of E. Brontë.
1849	Cavour is Minister of the Piedmont. The march of the French on Rome. Millet settles in the village of Barbizon. Daumier: *Les Fugitifs*. Delacroix: *Les Femmes d'Alger*. Courbet: *L'Après-Midi à Ornans*. Gustave Flaubert: *La Tentation de Saint-Antoine*. Kierkegaard: *The Sickness unto Death*. Death of Chopin and Edgar Allen Poe.

1850	Böcklin is in Italy. Labrouste constructs the Bibliothèque Sainte-Geneviève. Hugo: *Le Burg à la Croix*. Corot: *La Danse des Nymphes*. Millet: *Le Semeur*. Courbet: *Un Enterrement à Ornans*. The Goncourts found their *Journal*. Dickens: *David Copperfield*. Death of Balzac.
1851	First Universal Exposition held in London. Louis Napoleon's coup d'état in France. Singer invents the sewing machine. Verdi: *Rigoletto*. Brahms starts composing the piano recitals. Nerval: *Voyage en Orient*. Leconte de Lisle: *Poèmes antiques*. Barbey d'Aurevilly: *Une Vieille Maîtresse*. Labiche: *Un Chapeau de paille d'Italie*. Herman Melville: *Moby-Dick*. Death of Daguerre and of Turner.
1852	France occupies Senegal. Founding of the Bon Marché department store in Paris. Visconti works on his additions to the Louvre. Rude: *Jeanne d'Arc*. Wagner: *The Ring of the Nebelung*. Gautier: *Emaux et Camées*. Lamartine: *Graziella*. Dumas, fils: *La Dame aux Camélias*. Turgenev: *The Hunting Sketches*. Death of Gogol.
1853	Russo-Turkish War. Haussman appointed prefect of the Department of the Seine. Saint-Saëns: 1st Symphony. Verdi: *La Traviata*. Hugo: *Les Châtiments*. Renan: *La Vie de Jésus*.
1854	The Crimean War. Baltard constructs Les Halles in Paris. Nerval: *Les Filles de Feu, Les Chimères*. Augier: *Le Gendre de Monsieur Poirier*. Viollet-le-Duc: *Dictionnaire Raisonné de l'Architecture Français*.
1855	Exposition Universelle in Paris. Pissarro, born in the Antilles in 1830, arrives in Paris. Gounod: *Messe de Sainte-Cécile*. Nerval: *Aurélia*. Gobineau: *Essai sur l'Inégalité des Races Humaines*. Walt Whitman: *Leaves of Grass*. Death of Rude, of Charlotte Brontë and of Kierkegaard.
1856	Discovery of the Neanderthal man. Berlioz takes his post at the Institut. Death of Schumann and of Heine.

1857	Delacroix takes his post at the Institut. Daubigny: *Le Printemps*. Courbet: *Les Demoiselles de la Seine*. Millet: *Les Glaneuses*. Public proceedings against *Madame Bovary* and *Les Fleurs du Mal*. Death of Auguste Comte and of Musset.
1858	*Monet meets Boudin, who encourages him to work on landscape painting. Until then, Monet had done nothing but caricatures, for which he had garnered some local fame and which provided him with a modest living.* England colonizes the Indies. Completion of the Bois de Boulogne in Paris and start of improvement works on Vienna's Ring Strasse. Berlioz: *Les Troyens*. Offenbach: *Orphée aux Enfers*. Gautier: *Le Roman de la Momie*. Octave Feuillet: *Le Roman d'un Jeune Homme Pauvre*. Proudhon: *De la Justice dans la Révolution et dans l'Eglise*.
1859	*Monet sets out for Paris (in May). Gets advice from Troyon, famous painter of animals. Meets Pissarro at the Académie Suisse. The Brasserie des Martyrs, mecca of all young painters, is one of his favorite haunts.* First oil wells are being dug in the U.S. Military intervention in Italy; Austrian defeats in Magenta and Solferino. Ingres: *Le Bain Turc*. Millet: *L'Angelus*. Rossetti: *Dantis Amor*. Gounod: *Faust*. Wagner: *Tristan und Isolde*. Hugo: *La Légende des Siècles*. Ponson du Terrail: *Les Exploits de Rocambole*. Death of Thomas de Quincy.
1860	*Monet paints landscape in Champigny-sur-Marne. Is sent to Algeria for his military service.* A liberal monarchy. Prince Napoleon's Maison Pompeienne in Paris. Degas: *Jeunes Spartiates S'Excerçant à la Lutte*. Baudelaire: *Les Paradis Artificiels*. Labiche: *Le Voyage de Monsieur Perrichon*. Turgenev: *First Love*. Death of Schopenhauer.
1861	Creation of the Parliament in Italy. Abolition of serfdom in Russia. Start of the Civil War in the U.S. Founding of the Boer Republic in the Transvaal. Cézanne is in Paris, where he meets Pissarro at the Académie Suisse. Delacroix completes his paintings in the Saint-Sulpice. Garnier starts work on the Paris Opéra. Michelet: *La Mer*.

1862

Monet completes his military service and returns to his family in Normandy. Works at Saint-Adresse with Boudin. Meets Jongkind. In the fall, goes to Paris to study at the atelier of Gleyre, famous "official" painter, specialized in historical subjects. Makes friends with Bazille, Sisley and Renoir.

French expedition in Mexico. Bismarck president of the Council of Prussia. Pasteur experiments with fermentation. Manet: *Lola de Valence.* Liszt: *La Légende de St Elizabeth de Hongrie.* Leconte de Lisle: *Poèmes Barbares.* Hugo: *Les Misérables.*

1863

Monet and his friends work "on the motif" at Chailly, in the Fontainebleau forest.

Salon des Refusés. Gautier: *Le Capitaine Fracasse.* Fromentin: *Domenique.* Death of Alfred de Vigny, of Thackeray, of Grimm and of Delacroix.

1864

Monet meets Courbet. Spends the summer and fall in Honfleur. Works alongside Bazille.

Founding of the 1st Workers' International. Meissonnier: *1814.* Fantin-Latour: *Hommage à Delacroix.* Corot: *Souvenir de Mortefontaine.* Gounod: *Mireille.* Offenbach: *La Belle Hélène.* The Goncourts: *Renée Mauperin.* Labiche: *La Cagnotte.* Erkmann-Chatrian: *L'Ami Fritz.*

1865

Monet sets up shop in Bazille's studio, 5 Rue de Furstemberg. Exhibits at the Salon. Le Déjeuner sur l'Herbe *in Chailly.*

Renoir and Sisley are in Marlotte. Union victory in the U.S. and slavery is abolished. Manet's *Olympia* stirs scandal. Degas: *Les Malheurs de la Ville d'Orléans.* Gustave Moreau: *Jeune Fille Portant la Tête d'Orphée.* Rimsky-Korsakov: *First Symphony.* The Goncourts: *Germinie Lacerteux.* Jules Verne: *De la Terre à la Lune.*

1866

Monet paints scenes of Paris. Exhibits at the Salon Portrait de Camille, *noted by Zola. Works in Ville-d'Avray and in Honfleur:* Terrasse prés du Havre.

Austro-Prussian War. Carpeaux: *Le Triomphe de Flore.* Manet: *Le Fifre.* Bazille: *Réunion de Famille.* Offenbach: *La Vie Parisienne.* Tchaikovsky: *Song of Winter Symphony.* Verlaine: *Poèmes Saturniens.* Hugo: *Les Travailleurs de la Mer.* Dostoyevsky: *Crime and Punishment.*

1867	*Monet, stripped of all funds, returns to his family in Saint-Adresse, but Camille must remain in Paris, where she gives birth to their son Jean. Bazille offers to put him up in 1 Rue Visconti.* Maximilian executed in Mexico. Creation of the Buttes-Chaumont park in Paris. Saint-Saëns: *Quintette.* Verdi: *Don Carlos.* Borodine: *1st Symphonie.* Mallarmé: *Hérodiade.* The Goncourts: *Manette Salomon.* Michelet finishes his *Histoire de France.* Death of Ingres, of Théodore Rousseau and of Baudelaire.
1868	*Monet passes his days in Bonnières-sur-Seine, Fécamp and Etretat.* Foundation of the Société libre in Brussels. Completion of the Vincennes park. Labrouste finishes the great reading room at the Bibliothèque Nationale in Paris. Monet: *Portrait de Zola.* Degas: *Mademoiselle Fiocre dans la Ballet de la Source.* Grieg: *Piano Concerto.* Mussorgsky: *Boris Godunov.* Zola: *Thérèse Raquin.* Daudet: *Le Petit Chose.* Post-humous publication of Baudelaire's *Curiosités Esthétiques.* Dostoyevsky: *The Idiot.* Death of Rossini.
1869	*Monet settles in Bougival. Works with Renoir at "La Grenouillère".* Vatican council. Opening of the Suez Canal. Transcontinental ties with the U.S. Carpeaux: *La Danse.* Puvis de Chavannes: decoration of the Musée de Marseille. Verlaine: *Les Fêtes Galantes.* Lautréamont: *Les Chants de Maldoror.* Flaubert: *L'Education Sentimentale.* Death of Berlioz, Lamartine, Sainte-Beuve.
1870	*Monet and Camille get married. The war catches him by surprise in Trouville, where he is working, and he flees to London where Daubigny introduces him to the art dealer Durand-Ruel.*
1871	*London. Passes through Holland on his return to France. Settles in Argenteuil.* German victory over France. The Paris Commune. William I, emperor of Germany. Foundation of the national music society in Paris. Verdi: *Aida.* Rimbaud: "Le bateau ivre."
1872	*Monet paints* Impression: Soleil Levant *in Le Havre.* Fantin-Latour: *Un Coin de Table.* Degas: *La Femme à la Potiche.* Bizet: *L'Arlésienne.* Déroulède: *Le Chant du Soldat.* Charles Cros: *Le Coffret de Santal.* Daudet: *Tartarin de Tarascon.*

1873

Monet meets painter Gustave Caillebotte. Rigs his "atelier-bateau" for painting on the Seine.
Proclamation of the Spanish Republic. Manet: *Le Bon Bock.* Cézanne: *La Maison du Pendu.* Berthe Morisot: *Le Berceau.* Rimbaud: *Une Saison en Enfer.* Corbière: *Les Amours Jaunes.* Richepin: *La Chanson des Gueux.* Death of Manzoni.

1874

Monet is helped financially by Manet.
*First exhibition of the Impressionists held by the photographer Nadar in Boulevard des Capucines. Monet shows his Im-*pression: Soleil Levant, *which was the source of the group's name.*
Bizet: *Carmen.* Verdi: *Requiem.* Verlaine: *Romances sans Paroles.* Hugo: *Quatre-Vingt Treize.* Barbey d'Aurevilly: *Les Diaboliques.* Death of Michelet.

1875

Camille falls ill. Monet suffers great hardships.
Ratification of the constitution of the Third Republic of France. J.P. Laurens: *L'Excommunication de Robert le Pieux.* Saint-Saëns: *La Danse Macabre.* Grieg: *Peer Gynt.* Zola: *La Faute de l'Abbé Mouret.* Rimbaud: *Les Illuminations.* Death of Bizet, Fromentin, Labrouste, Carpeaux, Millet, Barye.

1876

Monet meets amateur Chocquet. Stays at collector Hoschedé's home in the Château de Montgeron. Gare Saint-Lazare series.
Second Impressionist Exhibition held by Durand-Ruel, Rue Le Peletier.
Bell invents the telephone. Renoir: *La Moulin de la Galette.* Sisley: *La Seine à Marly.* Brahms: *Symphony no. 1.* Tchaikovsky: *Swan Lake.* Mallarmé: "L'Après-Midi d'un Faune." Duranty: *La Nouvelle Peinture.* Death of Diaz, Corot, Georges Sand.

1877

Monet again visits Montgeron. Paints in Paris through the winter. Third Impressionist Exhibition held in 6 Rue Le Peletier.
France occupies the Congo. MacMahon's coup d'état in France fails. Edison uses the phonograph. Rodin: *L'Age d'Airin.* Degas: *Aux Ambassadeurs.* Saint-Saëns: *Samson et Delila.* Zola: *L'Assomoir.* Tolstoy: *Anna Karenina.* Death of Courbet.

1878

Monet settles in Vetheuil, on the banks of the Seine. Birth of Michel. Bankruptcy of the collector Hoschedé, whose family moves in with Monet.
Victoria is the Empress of the Indies. Puvis de Chavannes decorates the Panthéon in Paris. Gervex: *Rolla*. Brahms: *Violin Concerto*. Duret: *Les Peintres Impressionistes*. Death of Daubigny.

1879

Death of Camille. Particularly harsh winter; Monet paints the breaking up of the ice on the Seine. Fourth Impressionist Exhibition, 28 Avenue de l'Opéra.
Founding of the French socialist party by Jules Guesde. Pasteur discovers vaccines. Lalo: *Le Roi d'Ys*. Rimsky-Korsakov: *Night in May*. Smetana: *My Fatherland*. Huysmans: *Les Soeurs Vatard*. Ibsen: *The Dollhouse*. Death of Viollet-le-Duc, Daumier.

1880

Solo exhibition by Monet in the editorial offices of the journal La Vie Moderne, *made available to him by publisher Charpentier. Fifth Impressionist Exhibition, 10 Rue des Pyramides. Falling out between Degas and Monet.*
The Jesuits are expelled from France. Creation of the museum of decorative arts. Lefuel completes his additions to the Louvre. Bartholdi: *Le Lion de Belfort*. Mahler: *First Symphonic Song Cycle*. Mussorgsky: *Songs and Dances of Death*. Dvoràk: *Symphony no. 6*. Verlaine: *Sagesse*. Zola: *Nana*. Maupassant: *Boule de Suif*. Death of Flaubert, Eliot and Offenbach.

1881

Monet paints "sur le motif" at Vetheuil and Fécamp. He settles with Madame Hoschedé in Poissy. Sixth Impressionist Exhibition, 35 Boulevard des Capucines.
Tunisia becomes a French colony. Alexander II is assassinated in Russia. Start of work on the Panama Canal. Manet: *Le Bar des Folies Bergères*. Renoir: *Le Déjeuner des Canotiers*. Redon: *L'Araignée Souriante*. Massenet: *Hérodiade*. Vincent d'Indy: *Wallenstein*. Huysmans: *En Ménagé*. Maupassant: *Une Parite de Campagne*. Anatole France: *Le Crime de Sylvestre Bonnard*. Death of Dostoyevsky and Mussorgsky.

1882

Monet visits Varangeville, Dieppe and Purville. Seventh Impressionist Exhibition, 251 Rue Saint Honoré.
Laws on primary school education in France. Settlement of the British in Egypt. Wagner: *Parsifal*. Taine: *Philosophie de l'Art*. D'Annunzio: *Canto Nuovo*. Death of Emerson, Rossetti.

159

1883

Solo exhibition by Monet organized by Durand-Ruel. He settles in Giverny in May, in a house that he will buy in 1890. Trip to Provence with Renoir. They visit Cézanne in L'Estaque.
French troops occupy Madagascar. First electrical lines covering long distances. Ensor: *Masques.* Delibes: *Lakmé.* Maupassant: *Une Vie.* Loti: *Mon Frère Yves.* Villier de l'Isle-Adam: *Contes Cruels.* Stevenson: *Treasure Island.* Deaths of Manet, Gustave Doré, Wagner, Marx and Turgenev.

1884

Monet makes a lengthy visit to Bordighera, and then to Menton.
Franco-Chinese War. Union law in France. Belgium comes to power in the Congo. First electrical tramway. Detaille and Neuville: *Diorama: Le Soir de Rezonville.* Seurat: *Une Baignade.* Gustave Moreau: *Les Chimères.* Massenet: *Manon.* Debussy: *Apparition.* Moréas: *Les Syrtes.* Daudet: *Sapho.* Huysmans: *A Rebours.* Montépin: *La Porteuse de Pain.* Death of Smetana.

1885

Monet has a falling out with Durand-Ruel. Exhibits at the Georges Petit gallery.
Pasteur develops the rabies vaccination. Van Gogh: *Les Mangeurs de Pommes de Terre.* Laforgue: *Les Complaintes.* Becque: *La Parisienne.* Zola: *Germinal.* Death of Hugo and of Vallès.

1886

Monet meets Gustave Geffroy in Belle-Ile. Trip to Noirmoutier with Octave Mirbeau. Eighth and last Impressionist Exhibition, Rue Laffitte.
The Irish question in England. Bartholdi: *La Liberté Eclairant le Monde.* Rodin: *Le Baiser, La pensée.* Degas: *Le Tub.* Seurat: *Un Dimanche à la Grande Jatte.* Satie: *Ogives.* Zola: *L'Oeuvre.* Loti: *Pêcheurs d'Islande.* Bloy: *Le Désespéré.* Moréas: *Manifeste du Symbolisme.* Death of Liszt, Monticelli.

1887

Organization of the Indo-Chinese General Union. Formation of the "Nabis" group. Renoir: *Les Grandes Baigneuses.* Van Gogh: *Le Père Tanguy.* Chabrier: *Le Roi Malgré Lui.* Debussy: *Printemps.* Verdi: *Othello.* Rimsky-Korsakov: *Capriccio Espagnol.* Antoine founds the Théâtre Libre.

1888

Monet travels widely, to Antibes, London, Etretat.
First gasoline engine. Van Gogh and Gauguin are in Arles.
Detaille: *Le Rêve*. Gauguin: *La Vision Après le Sermon*.
Sérusier: *Paysage du Bois d'Amour*. Eric Satie: *Les Gymnopédies*. Debussy: *Deux Arabesques*. Richard Strauss: *Don Juan*. Mahler: *Symphony no. 1*. Sully Prudhomme: *Le Bonheur*. Jarry: *Ubu Roi*. Death of Labiche.

1889

Trip to the Creuse region. Exhibits with Rodin at the Georges Petit gallery.
Organization of the 2nd Workers' International. The Eiffel Tower in Paris. Puvis de Chavanne decorates the Sorbonne.
Gauguin: *La Demoiselle Elue*. Verlaine: *Parallèlement*.
Bourget: *Le Disciple*. Claudel: *Tête d'Or*. Bergson: *Essai sur les Données Immédiates de la Conscience*. Maeterlinck: *Serres Chaudes*.
Death of Barbey d'Aurevilly, Villier de l'Isle-Adam.

1890

Poplars and Haystacks series. Additions to the Giverny garden.
Bismarck's fall in Germany. First airplane flight by Ader.
First automobiles. Cézanne: *Les Jouers de Cartes*. Redon: *Les Yeux Clos*. Seurat: *Le Chahut*. Charpentier: *Impression d'Italie*. Chausson: *Symphonie*. Wilde: *Portrait of Dorian Gray*. Death of Franck and van Gogh.

1891

Exhibition in May organized by Durand-Ruel. Visit to London.
Start of construction of the Trans-Siberian railway.
Gauguin's first voyage to Tahiti. Maurice Denis: *Mystère Catholique*. Edvard Munch: *A Spring Day in Rue Karl Johan*.
Fauré: *Cinq Mélodies de Venise*. Eric Satie: *Gnossiennes*.
Barrès: *Le Jardin de Bérénice*. Claudel: *La Ville*. Huysmans: *La-Bas*. Rodenbach: *Le Règne du Silence*. Death of Melville, Jongkind, Meissonier and Seurat.

1892

Monet and Madame Hoschedé get married. Exhibition organized by Durand-Ruel.
Leon XIII's encyclic. Panama scandal in France. Péladan founds the Salon des Rose-Croix. Foundation of the Secession group in Munich.
Lautrec: *La Goulue*. Bonnard: *Intérieur*. Roussel: *Femme au Peignoir Bleu*. Massenet: *Werther*. Saint-Pol Roux: *Le Reposoirs de la Procession*. Zola: *La Débâcle*. Rodenbach: *Bruges la Morte*. Maeterlinck: *Pelléas et Mélisande*. Death of Renan.

1893

Rouen Cathedral series.
Miners' strike in England. Caillebotte bequeaths his collection to the French state. H.E. Cross: *Venice*. Munch: *The Cry*. Verdi: *Falstaff*. Eric Satie: *Les Préludes*. Debussy: *Quatuor*. Hérédia: *Les Trophées*. Samain: *Au Jardin de l'Infant*. A. France: *La Rôtisserie de la Reine Pédauque*. Death of Taine, Maupassant, Gounod and Tchaikovsky.

1894

Cézanne meets Rodin, Clemenceau and Geoffroy at Giverny.
Start of the Dreyfus Affair in France. Le Douanier Rousseau: *La Guerre*. Munch: *Anguish*. Debussy: *Prélude à l'Après-Midi d'un Faune*. Pierre Louÿs: *Chanson de Bilitis*. Barrès: *Du Sang, de la Volupté et de la Mort*. Jules Renard: *Poil de Carotte*. Claudel: *L'Echange*. Death of Chabrier, Leconte de Lisle, Stevenson, Caillebotte.

1895

Monet travels to Norway. Exhibition at the Durand-Ruel gallery.
Michelin improves tires for automobiles. Lumière cinematograph. Rodin: *Les Bourgeois de Calais*. Ravel: *La Habanera*. Valéry: *Introduction à la Methode de Léonard de Vinci*. Verhaeren: *Les Ville Tantaculaires*. Freud: *Studien uber Hysterie*. Death of Berthe Morisot, Dumas fils.

1896

Monet in Varangeville. The "Cliffs".
Marconi invents the wireless telegraph. Inauguration in Paris of the Bing gallery. Guimard: *Castel Beranger*. Levy-Dhurmer: *Salomé*. Puccini: *La Bohême*. Marcel Proust: *Les Plaisirs et les Jours*. Bergson: *Matière et Mémoire*. Death of Verlaine and of E. de Goncourt.

1897

Monet stays in Pourville.
Foundation of the Zionist movement. Queen Victoria's jubilee. Formation of the Viennese Secession. Rodin: *Balzac*. Le Douanier Rousseau: *La Bohémienne Endormie*. Boldini: *Robert de Montesquieu*. Mallarmé: *Un Coup de Dés*. Gide: *Les Nourritures Terrestres*. Rostand: *Cyrano de Bergerac*. Death of Daudet and of Brahms.

1898

Monet exhibits at the Georges Petit gallery.
Spanish-American War in Cuba. Maillol: *La Vague*. Fauré: *Pelléas et Mélisande*. Samain: *Aux Flancs du Vase*. Huysmans: *La Cathédral*. Deaths of Charles Garnier, Puvis de Chavannes, Mallarmé and Rodenbach.

1899	*Unveiling of the "water lily pond" in Monet's garden. The London series.* Formation of the Berlin Secession. Vallotton: *Baignade à Etretat*. Schönberg: *Verklarte Nacht*. Debussy: *Nocturnes*. Jarry: *L'Amour Absolu*. Signac: *D'Eugène Delacroix au Néo-Impressionisme*. Milosz: *Poèmes des Décadents*. Death of Sisley.
1900	*Monet in London. Clemenceau's visit to Giverny.* Paris, Exposition Universelle. French art Centennial. Assassination of Umberto I in Italy. Formation of the Labour Party in England. Guimard constructs the Grand-Palais, the Gare D'Orsay, and Métro entrances in Paris. Bourdelle: *Beethoven*. Munch: *The Dance of Life*. Puccini: *La Tosca*. Octave Mirbeau: *Journal d'une Femme de Chambre*. Jarry: *Ubu Enchaîné*. Death of Nietzsche and of Ruskin.
1901	*Monet in London.* Ravel: *Jeu d'Eau*. Anna de Noailles: *Le Coeur Innombrable*. Maurras: *Anthinea*. Maeterlinck: *La Vie des Abeilles*. Deaths of Böcklin, Lautrec, Verdi.
1902	*Monet stays in Brittany.* Méliès: *Le Voyage dans la Lune*. Debussy: *Pelléas et Mélisande*. Gide: *L'Immoraliste*. Romain Rolland: *Le Quatorze Juillet*. Death of Dalou and of Zola.
1903	*Monet buys a car for family excursions in the Giverny region. Finishes the London paintings from memory.* Perret constructs in building in Rue Franklin in Paris. Debussy: *Jardins sous la Pluie*. Schönberg: *Pelléas et Mélisande*. Octave Mirbeau: *Les Affaires Sont les Affaires*. Deaths of Gauguin, Pissarro, Whistler.
1904	*Monet paints his* Water Lilies. *Exhibits his London series at Durand-Ruel's gallery.* Start of the Anglo-French *entente cordiale*. Russo-Japanese War. Defeat of the Russian navy. "La Cage aux Fauves" (Salon d'Automne). Tony Garnier: *La Cité Industrielle*. Puccini: *Madame Butterfly*. Samain: *Polyphème*. Pierre Loti: *Vers Ispahan*. Death of Fantin-Latour.

1905

Monet works exclusively on his Water Lilies.
Separation of the Church and State in France. Uprisings in Russia. Frantz-Jourdan constructs the Samaritaine building in Paris. Le Douanier Rousseau: *La Noce.* Debussy: *La Mer.* Death of Jules Verne.

1906

Monet continues to work exclusively on his Water Lilies.
Formation of the Moslem League in India. Gandhi preaches passive resistance in South Africa. In Teheran, the Iranian revolution is broadly supported by a religious movement. Bergson: *L'Evolution Créatrice.* Rouault: *Olympias.* Van Dongen: *The Clown.* Derain: *Le Pont de Westminster.* Claudel: *Portage de Midi.* Death of Cézanne.

1907

Monet's sight problems begin.
Socialist Convention in Amiens. Start of widespread union activity and the use of strike tactics. 740,000 Chinese are converted to Catholicism.
Picasso: *Les Demoiselles d'Avignon.* Robert Delauney: *Portrait de Wilhelm Uhde.* Matisse: *La Coiffure.* Braque: *Paysage à l'Estaque.* Kubin: *The Couple.* Death of Jarry.

1908

Monet travels to Venice.
Construction of the Woolworth Building, giving rise to the myth of the skyscraper. Bonnard: *La Loge.* Dufy: *Paysage de l'Estaque.* La Fresnaye: *L'Après-Midi d'un Faune.* Valery Larbaud: *Barnabooth.*

1909

Monet's Water Lilies *exhibited at the Durand-Ruel gallery.*
The Futurist manifesto is published. Brancusi: *La Musa Addormentata.* Picabia: *Caoutchouc.* Robert Delauney: *Saint-Severin.* Klimt: *The Kiss.* Jawlensky: *Young Girl with Peonies.* Suzanne Valadon: *Après le Bain.* André Gide: *La Porte Etroite.*

1910

Monet enlarges his water lily pond in his Giverny garden.
Picasso: *Portrait de D. H. Kahnweiler.* Léger: *La Noce.* Emil Nolde: *The Dance of the Golden Calf.* Foundation of Der Sturm in Berlin. Death of Jules Renard.

1911	*Death of Alice Hoschedé-Monet.* Matisse: *La Fenêtre Bleu.* Chagall: *Hommage à Apollinaire.* De Chirico: *L'Enigma dell'Ora.* Marquet: *Nu à Contre Jour.* Egon Shiele: *Two Sleeping Girls.*
1912	*Exhibition of the Venice series at the Bernheim-Jeune gallery.* "Blaue Reiter" movement in Munich. Delauney: *Les Fenêtres.* August Mack: *Jardin Zoologique.* Mondrian: *Apple Tree in Bloom.* Blaise Cendrars: *Les Pâques à New York.* Charles Péguy: *Tapisseries.*
1913	Kupka: *Plans Verticaux Bleues et Rouges.* Modigliani: *Testa.* Guillaume Apollinaire: *Alcools.* Blaise Cendrars: *Prose du Transsibérien.*
1914	*Death of Jean Monet. Claude Monet has a new studio built to work on a huge composition of water lilies.* Outbreak of World War I. Kirchner: *Berlin Street Scene.* Klee: *Southern Garden.* Duchamp-Villon: *Le Cheval.* Magnelli: *Virginia.* Death of Alain-Fournier, Juarès, Péguy.
1915	Marcel Duchamp: *La Mariée Mise à Nue par ses Célibataires Mêmes.* Malevitch: *Suprematism.* Apollinaire: *Case d'Armons.* Romain Rolland: *Au dessus de la Mêlée.*
1916	The French attack in Picardie. First dada demonstrations in Zurich. Grosz: *The City.* Henri Barbusse: *Le Feu.* Death of Verhaeren.
1917	United States involvement in the war. The Russian Revolution. Foundation of the "Der Stijl" movement. Kokoschka: *The Friends.* Modigliani: *Portrait de Cendrars.* Max Jacob: *Le Cornet à Dés.* Death of Octave Mirbeau and of Degas.
1918	Defeat of the Germans in the Battle of the Marne. End of hostilities. Apollinaire: *Calligrammes.* Picabia: *Poèmes de la Fille sans Mère.* Death of Apollinaire.

1919	The Treaty of Versailles. Foundation of the "Bauhaus." R. Wiene: *Le Cabinet du Docteur Caligari*. Juan Gris: *Nature Morte*. Foundation of the journal *Littérature* by André Breton, Philippe Soupault and Louis Aragon.
1920	*Plan drawn up for the construction of a building in the Rodin museum park, to house Monet's Water Lilies series.* Congress in Tours (France) determines the break between communists and socialists. Grosz: *Daum Marries*. Schwitters: *Merz* paintings. Picabia: *La Saint Vierge*. First exhibition of Max Ernst's works in Paris. Tristan Tzara: *Cinéma Calendrier du Coeur Abstrait*. Cocteau: *Poésies*. Post-humous publication of Aragon's *Feu de Joie*.
1921	Lenin applies the new economic laws in Russia. Breton and Soupault: *Les Champs Magnétiques*.
1922	*In the end the "Orangerie" in the Tuileries is chosen for the permanent exhibition of the Water Lilies.* Mussolini breaks the general strike in Italy. Max Ernst: *Oedipus Rex*. Valéry: *Charmes*. Joyce: *Ulysses*. Le Corbusier makes his first concrete construction. Death of Marcel Proust.
1923	*Monet's cataract is operated on.* Man Ray: *De quoi Ecrire*. Colette: *La Maison de Claudine*. Jules Romains: *Knock*. Death of Radiguet, Barrès, Pierre Loti.
1924	France recognizes the Soviet Union. Surrealist manifesto. Eisenstein: *The Battleship Potemkin*. Death of Anatole France.
1925	Trotsky removed from his office in the USSR. Paris Exposition Universelle. Otto Dix: *Berlin Prostitutes*.
1926	*Giverny, 6 December: Monet dies.*